I0759583

YOU
HAVE THE
POWER
WITHIN
YOURSELF

ILLUSTRATIONS BY
MIRA NURDIANTI

INSTANT WITCH

THE BEGINNER'S GUIDE

MEGAN ARCHER

Quadrille

CONTENTS

Welcome, Curious One

If you've picked up this book, it's likely that you are wondering where to begin on your magickal journey. Or perhaps you are an advanced practitioner looking for a fresh take on the craft, or maybe you are a witch hunter, looking for evidence. Whoever you are, I hope to provide a safe space for you to harness and grow your magick.

Magick permeates the world around us – if only you know where to look. You've probably made a birthday wish on a candle or knocked on wood to avoid misfortune. Maybe you've experienced a coincidence that can't quite be explained. A simple remark made in passing could very well end up manifesting unintended consequences. A key concept of witchcraft is the interconnectivity of the natural world. As witches, we work with these forces and learn to influence them with our will.

Who am I, to preach such things? I'm Megan, an eclectic, chaotic, solitary first-generation practitioner. By the end of this book, you will know what each of these terms means, and will even have the knowledge to define yourself – although I urge you to not get too caught up in the terminology because that can be overwhelming, and practically it really doesn't matter whether you're a 'green' witch or 'hedge' witch. Ethnically, I am European and Southeast Asian (Thai). My practice similarly fuses both Eurocentric and Asian spirituality, with a sprinkling of folk magick. My mission is to make witchcraft more easily digestible, while adapting it to modern times. Working with magick has vastly improved my life, and I endeavour to change yours similarly.

My fascination with the occult started early. My dad taught me how to read tarot when I was ten years old. I remember the first time I gave a prediction that was spot-on – the addictive rush of truly helping someone. From there, it was a slippery slope of astrology readings – and countless episodes of *Buffy the Vampire Slayer*.

I began studying witchcraft in earnest, like many, during the pandemic of 2020. With the world ablaze, turning to magick seemed reasonable. I dabbled in the law of attraction before turning to the harder stuff – real witchcraft. One thing soon became glaringly obvious: there is a vast ocean of magickal knowledge to drink from. No one can seem to agree on where to start or even what to call it! That is both the beauty and the weakness of witchcraft. It's quite literally a craft, not a science. Practising witchcraft requires you to both suspend your disbelief and commit to full belief in your own power.

WITCHY KNOWLEDGE - Who put the k in magick?

So what's with the k, anyway? The 'k' was added by Aleister Crowley in the mid-1900s to differentiate ritual magick from stage magic. Because of Crowley's questionable nature (occultist, libertine, devil-raiser and all-round bad boy), some are against this spelling. But I like the k, so I've used it in this book.

Understanding this power can be daunting. There are countless methods and hundreds of years of witchcraft to explore. The fun part is that you will always be a student – there is more to learn than anyone could possibly absorb in a single lifetime. But you need to start somewhere, and that's what this book is about. It is designed to guide you through core tenets of witchcraft one by one, and to give you a secure foundation from which you can continue on your quest for knowledge. While it is impossible to cover every aspect of witchcraft, I aim to give you all the tools you need to pave your own path.

This book is written with the beginner in mind; there will be no unattainable rituals with 25 different ingredients. You will learn everything from spells for enchanting your morning coffee, to working with the power of the Moon – realistic ways to incorporate magick, both big and small, into your life. This book is the guidance I wish I'd had when I was a younger witch, fresh-faced and just starting out. At the very least, it would have saved me from some poorly executed spells.

We will journey together through the foundations of witchcraft, breaking down the old stereotypes, collecting the tools we need, learning how to energetically align our homes, and much more. Come one, come all, and let's dive into the world of witchcraft together.

COME ONE, COME ALL, AND LET'S DIVE INTO THE WORLD OF WITCHCRAFT TOGETHER.

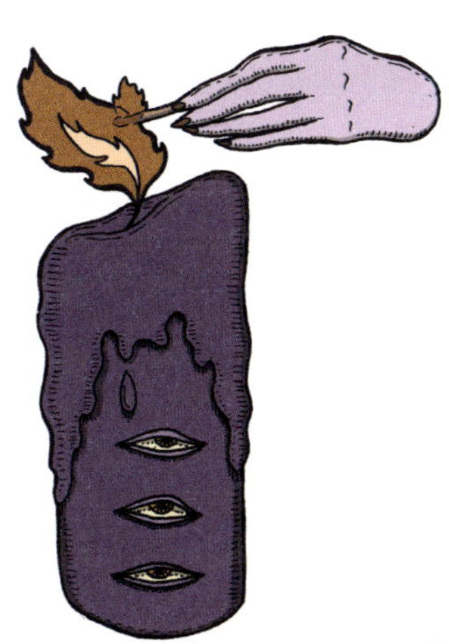

Witch Theory & Core Concepts

N
W
E
S

What is Witchcraft?

Learning the craft is a lifelong process. The instant you embark on the journey is the moment you commit to embracing your own power; that is just the start. Like everything in life, your practice will fluctuate. There will be periods when you're doing spells every day and months when you forget to refresh your altar. That's why it is important to find magick in the mundane: stirring your stew with intention; saying thank you to your favourite tree; hexing the man who catcalled you. Witchcraft is not always, or even usually, a fancy ceremonial ritual. It's more of a philosophy – a promise to honour and connect with the natural energies within.

In the past, witchcraft had a dark reputation; it was considered evil until very recently. There was even speculation that witches licked the devil's asshole (*Osculum infame* – look it up). If a little devil anilingus is all it takes to fly, I'm on board. Sadly, I haven't had the opportunity.

WITCHY KNOWLEDGE - Witchcraft got bad press

'A witch was described by four main characteristics: practising maleficium, or doing harm by supernatural means, flying, going to witches' gatherings, called covens, and having a pact with the devil.'

Richard A. Horsley (1979). *Who Were the Witches? The Social Roles of the Accused in the European Witch Trials.*

Today, we're taking back the term 'witch'. No longer does it imply having dealings with the devil or doing harm. Witchcraft itself is a neutral practice. Yes, it can be used to harm, but also to heal. Your world is what you make of it.

✷ TYPES OF WITCHCRAFT ✷

We love putting labels on things – categorizing them into perfect little boxes. You'll find many definitions of witchcraft – pick one or borrow from a few. Do whatever feels aligned to your energy. The witch police won't come for you.

INSTANT WITCH TIP – Make it yours

The following is my own understanding, based on practice and research. It is designed as a starting point and is certainly not all-encompassing. Different practitioners within each 'sect' will hold their own beliefs. Witchcraft is not like Christianity (in case that isn't obvious); there is no canon, no Bible equivalent. I encourage you to look up multiple sources on whatever topics interest you and follow what resonates. Below are a few relevant types of witchcraft, but it is certainly not an exhaustive list.

- **Traditional witchcraft:** What comes to mind when you hear the word 'witch'? Is it a woman, usually living alone in a remote cottage filled with hanging herbs? European in origin, folk magick was a tool of the oppressed to fight back against oppressors.

- **Eclectic witchcraft:** Eclectic witches are magickal chameleons. They don't confine themselves to one tradition but instead borrow from many. They learn mostly through trial and error, and what feels intuitive. They may impose some rules on themselves or none at all.

- **Chaos magick:** A modern tradition of magick originating in England in the 1970s, and a bit looser than eclectic witchcraft. Chaos witches do whatever they like. They might even invoke modern characters when performing spellwork: Jessica Rabbit for a love spell, for example.

- **Solitary witches:** If you are a solitary practitioner, you primarily work on your own. That does not mean you don't have any witchy friends. On the other hand, you may belong to a coven, a community of witches who practise their craft together. Today, with the power of the internet, it is easier than ever to find a coven.

CLOSET WITCH TIP – The broom closet

Witches may wish to practise in secret for one reason or another: a religious parent or conservative community, to name just two. It's not that long ago that they could be tortured or burned – so who can blame them for wanting to stay under the radar? Colloquially, we call this being 'in the broom closet'. At the time I'm writing this book, I am still in the broom closet to many of my family members. I guess the black cat's out of the bag now! If you're in the broom closet, don't fret. A whispered spell in your room at midnight can be just as potent as a Black Mass under the full moon. I've sprinkled some great tips for you throughout the book.

WITCHES MAY WISH TO PRACTISE IN SECRET FOR ONE REASON OR ANOTHER.

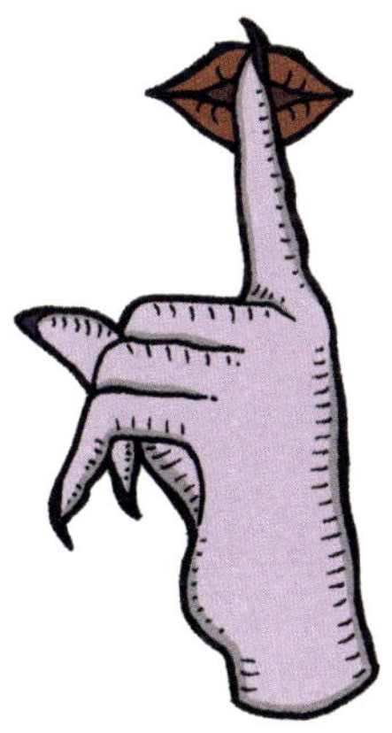

✷ CULTURAL APPROPRIATION ✷

As witches, we may take inspiration from many different sources, and dotted throughout this text are several concepts that have nothing to do with traditional witchcraft, which is primarily Eurocentric. For me, exploring witchcraft means examining concepts not just from the culture of my father, who has European heritage and is a hippie (which counts as pagan, in my opinion), but also from that of my mother, who is Southeast Asian and Buddhist. Incense, meditation and ancestral work are all key parts of my spiritual practice. And I address these concepts from a place of appreciation, not appropriation. When learning about another culture's traditions, it's important to come from a place of respect and curiosity.

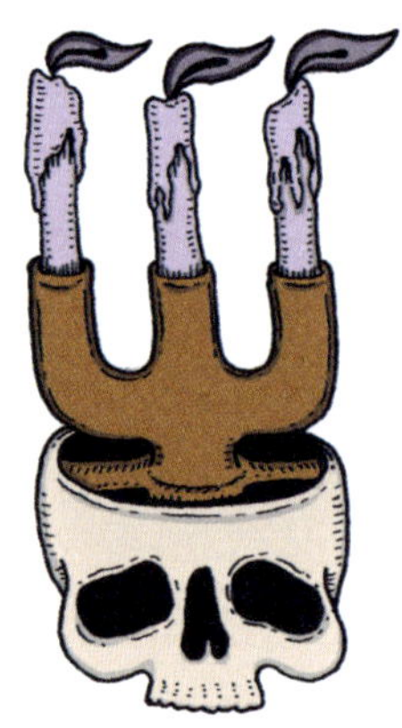

YOU CAN'T JUST TAKE YOUR WAY THROUGH LIFE.

✷ THE OLD GODS & THE NEW ✷

Working with a god or gods is not a requirement for being a witch. Christian witches and atheist witches alike rejoice! Find common ground! Be kind to each other. Deity work isn't mentioned much in this book, not because deity work is advanced or dangerous or anything like that, but because I don't do much of it. And it feels disingenuous to teach what I don't practise. The following explanations cover the topics I think you are likely to come across in your exploration of witchcraft, and therefore a brief note might be helpful.

THE GODDESS & THE HORNED GOD

Witches don't follow a single deity. In Wiccan mythos, the Goddess is seen as the source of creation, with the Horned God as her son-consort. They represent the creative female and male principles that are the complementary and essential parts of a balanced whole. The divine feminine Goddess nurtures, creates and receives. The divine masculine Horned God takes action, protects and leads.

OFFERINGS

You may want to make a small offering to your deity or guiding principle daily. That might involve saving the juiciest piece of chicken to give to your familiar (page 120), leaving out some berries for the birds or putting an extra plate on your altar (page 116). Consider the sensitivities of the recipient of your gift. When leaving an offering for a deity, do your research first. Some, like the Greek gods, will be offended by human offerings (meaning blood), but will appreciate animal offerings.

What you are aiming to achieve is a balance of receiving and giving. You can't just take your way through life. Many Buddhists believe you should do something kind before breakfast, and that concept fits well with a witch's philosophy.

THERE IS
NO CHEAT CODE
TO SPIRITUAL
ACTUALIZATION.

The Theory of Witchcraft

In this chapter, we will cover basic theories of witchcraft. You will get the first taste of harnessing your power and manipulating energy. Take your time working through this section. Once you have a solid understanding of energy work, move on.

Witchcraft at its core is influencing energy using will, working with (or sometimes against) the world around you to shape it to your liking. In today's society of constant stimulation, it can be tempting to skip the less glamorous basics, like meditation, and move on to more exciting things, like hexing. But without the proper baseline skills, your workings will be weak and unfocused.

Time spent strengthening your mental abilities will pay dividends. The more effort and focus you put into your craft, the more powerful you will become. That's the cold, hard truth. There is no cheat code to spiritual actualization. Witchcraft is a practice. As my old piano teacher would say, 'Practice doesn't make perfect – perfect practice does.'

One of the first things a new witch should do is get clear on their system of beliefs. Everyone has their own personal moral code. Hopefully, these values include things like freedom, happiness and justice.

✴ CONSENT ✴

Consent in witchcraft is a tricky beast. It is up to the practitioner whether they need someone's consent to practise on them. This may be a controversial take, but I will occasionally do a spell to 'nudge' someone in the right direction or to help them achieve a positive outcome, like a new job.

I recommend not doing spells that infringe upon the free will of others. For example, I would not recommend casting a love spell on a stranger. That's how you end up with a stalker...

For baneful workings, or workings meant to cause harm, consent goes out of the window. It is important to raise protections, and cover your crown while performing anything baneful. For more information, see pages 137–141.

✷ ENERGY ✷

Witches aim to tap in to the energy around us and shape it as we see fit. Everything is energy: the air we breathe, the food we eat, the cells in our bodies. Scientifically, energy is the ability to do work. In witchcraft, energy is the vital force both within and around us. English is the only language that does not have a specific term for this life-force energy – the difference between a living creature and a dead body. In Chinese tradition, this is called chi, or xi. The closest terms we have in English are spirit or aether.

Witchcraft requires both the raising and the control of this vital energy. Energy vibrates at different speeds. If you've ever noticed a 'vibe', you've noticed something's energy. Negative emotions, like sadness, are associated with low vibrations. Positive emotions, like love, are associated with high vibrations.

Energy ball exercise

This exercise is the basis of Tai Chi.

- Sit somewhere comfortable and take three deep breaths, inhaling energy up your spine.
- As you exhale, direct your focus to your hands. Rub your hands together, feeling this energy growing as you generate friction. Imagine the energy forming into a ball.
- Separate your hands while maintaining the energy ball. It may feel like magnets repelling each other or a cool tingling in your hands. If you feel nothing, start over.

- Once you've successfully created an energy ball, play around with it. Move it around. See if you can expand it, shrink it, make it stronger. Try to fill the room with it. When you've finished, clap your hands to dispel the energy ball.

STAGNANT ENERGY

While we may think of energy as electric and moving, it can also become stagnant. Stagnant energy is similar to a stagnant pond: sluggish, blocked and all together icky. Stagnant energy is nefarious and pervasive. As a witch, once you notice stagnation, it is your duty to unblock it. That is the double-edged sword of this work – once you see it, you can't unsee it.

Stagnant energy comes in many forms. It can live in your body in tense muscle tissue. It can live in your home as a dust bunny under the bed. It can even live in your brain as repeated negative thought patterns. Shadow work (pages 52–53) can help us shift these patterns and release stagnant energy.

ENERGETIC BURNOUT

As a new witch, it is tempting to start a million different spells and crafts, but if you do too much too fast, you risk an energetic burnout, especially if you start doing a load of mental work when you hadn't done any previously. Think of your energetic body as a muscle that can be trained with exercise but can also be injured by overwork.

Burnout looks different in everyone. You might feel depleted and overwhelmed. You might find it impossible to effectively raise energy. You might just feel like sitting on the couch and doing nothing.

If you notice burnout, take time off from new crafts. Try to finish what you have already started. The overwhelm from too many works-in-progress can be draining. If needed, take a few days off practising entirely. Spend as much time as you can in nature, away from screens. When you feel like yourself again, resume your craft.

AURAS

We all have an energetic field that extends several feet around us. Your aura is a combination of the physical, such as the perfumes you wear, and the metaphysical, such as the thoughts you think. When a person walks into a room and the vibration immediately shifts, you've sensed their aura. Some witches are even able to see coloured auras. If you don't have that ability, but would like to know the colour of your own aura, aura photography is a popular new offering at many metaphysical shops.

You can use your aura to quickly protect yourself in public. Just imagine your aura as being made up spikes. Visualize them protecting you, poking anyone who enters your space. When you do this, people will give you a wider berth than usual.

WHEN A PERSON WALKS INTO A ROOM AND THE VIBRATION IMMEDIATELY SHIFTS, YOU'VE SENSED THEIR AURA.

✷ TRADITIONAL CONCEPTS ✷

A concept of Wicca (more on that on page 78) is the idea that any energy you put out into the universe returns to you threefold. Personally, I think it's hogwash. Newton's third law states for every action, there is an equal and opposite reaction. If we could multiply energy three times, capitalism would've harnessed it somehow.

HARM TO NONE

Another concept from Wicca is that you can do what you will as long as you don't harm anyone. I don't buy in to that one, either. If there is injustice, sometimes we need to take matters into our own hands. This is your Libra bestie telling you it's okay to whip out that hex jar. Avoid harming *innocents*, sure. But certain individuals bring it upon themselves. As a witch, you hold the power to speed up their karma.

TRUE WILL

This is your 'why'. It's a concept borrowed from Thelema – an esoteric movement founded by Aleister Crowley in the early 1900s. The idea is that we all have a unique life purpose, but it can become obscured through old patterns and the ego. Observe how you spend your time. Do you call yourself a writer but haven't written in ages? Do you say you eat healthily but haven't had a home-cooked meal in weeks?

Do less of what drains you and more of what fills your cauldron. When you feel unmotivated or unclear, it is probably because you have drifted from your true will. When we connect back with our 'why' it is much easier to make productive progress in our lives.

✷ MEDITATION ✷

There is no substitute for the mindfulness practice of meditation – it is the one thing in witchcraft that is required. The better you are able to focus, the more powerful your spellwork will be. If meditation seems impossible, you need it more.

Meditation is not all staring at a wall in silence. Try doing a walking meditation in nature or even listening to a guided meditation. The important part is you take time (ideally daily) to clear your mind and centre yourself.

Grounding middle pillar meditation

The middle pillar exercise is a meditative exercise originating from the Hermetic Order of the Golden Dawn. Before performing magick, or whenever you need a little grounding, try this simple, informal version (with less chanting than the original).

- Start by sitting or standing, with your spine as straight as possible. Your eyes can be closed or open. I personally find it easier to focus when my eyes are open, as it stops the mind from racing.
- Take three deep breaths. Visualize yourself within a column of vibrant energy. It can be white, gold or any colour that resonates. Imagine the column extending infinitely in both directions. Envision it entering your body through your feet, and leaving your body through the top of your head.
- Now, picture a sphere of light approximately three metres (ten feet) above your head. As you breathe in, direct your breath up the pillar to the sphere of light. Hold the energy for a few seconds before exhaling.
- As you exhale, direct your breath downward and out through the bottoms of your feet (or spine). Repeat this process several times. As you inhale, imagine the light purifying you, and as you exhale, feel stagnant energy releasing.
- Do this as many times as you need, or until you feel properly grounded. This exercise puts you in the perfect state for spellwork and divination.

✷ MANIFESTATION ✷

Manifestation is bringing something tangible into your life through attraction, belief and action. You cannot manifest unless you meditate. Louder – for the people in the back – you cannot manifest unless you meditate. In Sanskrit, there is a term 'chitta vritti', which translates as 'the monkey mind'. The monkey mind is your mind, unregulated, and full of disjointed, seemingly uncontrollable thoughts. Through meditation, you can learn to master this chatter. Controlling the monkey mind allows us to find your true will. When you connect with your true will, you can better direct your life. You can do this by manifestation.

✷ VISUALIZATION ✷

Visualization is the ability to conjure an image in your mind's eye, forming a mental picture of an object, place or person that is not really there. Witches often use visualization during spellwork to direct energy. Visualizing something that doesn't yet exist in the physical realm is a powerful way to make it manifest. The sky's the limit when it comes to visualization. There is no budget involved, or even constraints like gravity.

Visualization exercise

The more you practise, the clearer your visualizations will become.

- Pick an object: something with details but not too complex, such as a key, candle or cup.
- Close your eyes, and picture the object in your mind. Turn it around, and view it from multiple angles. How much detail can you envision? Try focusing on it for several minutes.
- When you feel comfortable, move on to more complex objects. See how clearly you can summon the image of your chosen object after not visualizing it for a few hours.
- Next, try to maintain the visualization with your eyes open.

> INSTANT WITCH TIP – Take a break
>
> If you ever get a headache when doing a mental exercise, stop and take a break.

APHANTASIA

Aphantasia is a neurological condition that prevents visualization. If you are unable to visualize in the manner described on the previous page, try one of these alternative methods.

- Print off a picture.
- Draw a representation of the object.
- Invoke your other senses (touch, taste, smell, hearing). What does your end result feel like?

VISUALIZING SOMETHING THAT DOES NOT YET EXIST IN THE PHYSICAL REALM IS A POWERFUL WAY TO MAKE IT MANIFEST.

✷ DISCERNMENT ✷

The ability to judge, and trust that judgement, is known as discernment.

We are all born with different levels of discernment. As a child, you may have been told to suppress gut feelings and listen to your elders. Work to unlearn this habit and cultivate your discernment. Do not disregard personal experience simply because someone in a position of authority says something.

I have never trusted my gut and been wrong. On the flip side, every time I have ignored my instincts, it has ended badly.

✷ CLOSED PRACTICES ✷

Closed practices in witchcraft are limited to those born into them, or initiated into a certain group. For anyone else, they are 'closed', meaning not 'open' for use in your practice.

The most ubiquitous closed practice is smudging with white sage. Smudging itself is a specific prayer ritual performed by Native Americans. Using smoke to purify is open to all, but the terminology for this is 'smoke cleansing'. Do not refer to smoke cleansing as smudging, unless you are authorized to do the ritual of smudging.

White sage is a plant native to California, which risks being overharvested due to its appropriation by mainstream spirituality. Go to any big box store's spiritual section and you'll find dozens of white sage smudge bundles with questionable sourcing. Try smoke cleansing with white sage alternatives like juniper, rosemary or garden sage.

Hoodoo is another example of a closed practice. If you are not descended from an enslaved American, Hoodoo is off the table.

If you accidentally perform a closed practice, don't panic. You don't know what you don't know. Get rid of any closed tools immediately, either through burying them or gifting them to someone initiated into the practice. You can optionally offer a prayer to any spirits you may have insulted. And then don't do it again.

MAGICKAL TOOLS

ONLY WHAT YOU NEED

THE ONLY THING necessary for your magickal practice is yourself. You don't need to run out and buy a single thing before starting. The tools at a witch's disposal matter far less than determination and willpower. You can perform most spells with herbs you have on hand or even without herbs at all.

Traditionally, witches did not have metaphysical stores or online ordering available – they worked with what they had. You probably already own most of the items I'll describe here, or at least have something similar in your cabinets. Still, it can be fun to collect and use a variety of magickal tools. And if you're Venusian like me, you love shopping.

Mass-produced magickal items are readily available. When possible, though, opt for second-hand tools in estate sales, antique stores, second-hand stores and charity shops. You can even make a day of it with your thrifty, witch-minded friends. There's nothing more satisfying than finding the perfect mortar and pestle at an antique store going for a song.

Ideally, only use magickal items for magickal purposes. It may be tempting to grab your athame when you can't find scissors. Or your cauldron may look like a convenient punch bowl (that's how you end up with a rusty cauldron). If you use magickal items for mundane jobs, they may 'rebel' and break under mysterious circumstances.

Thoroughly clean any magickal items before using them, regardless of where you got them. Both store-bought and second-hand items collect energies on their way to you.

✷ CAULDRON ✷

When you think of witches, the image of a bubbling cauldron is not far behind. A cauldron is a fire-proof pot traditionally used for cooking over an open flame. They are sturdy pots, typically with three legs, a handle and a lid. Most often, cauldrons are made of cast iron. Cauldrons are symbolic of the womb, the divine feminine, and are associated with the water element. In witchcraft, cauldrons are primarily used for heating liquids, like candle wax, and burning things, like herb blends. Whether you need to make stew or burn your enemies, a cauldron has your back.

CLOSET WITCH TIP – Cauldron

A casserole dish (Dutch oven) works perfectly as a substitute for a cauldron.

✷ PENTACLE ✷

Pentacles and pentagrams are often confused. A pentagram is a five-pointed star, while a pentacle is a pentagram enclosed in a circle. The five points of a pentagram represent the four classical elements (earth, air, fire and water) and aether (spirit). Aether, introduced by the ancient Greek philosopher Aristotle, connects the other elements. Pentacles are considered symbols of protection. Sculpt a pentacle out of clay or wood to place on your altar (pages 116–117), or wear a pentacle pendant on your person.

✷ RITUAL BLADES ✷

ATHAME

An athame is a ritual knife used to direct energy. Traditionally, they are black-handled and double-edged. While they are knives, they are not generally used for cutting. Most commonly, they are used to cast a circle or otherwise channel energy.

BOLINE

A boline is a blade typically used for cutting. They are usually shaped like a sickle, and are white-handled. Unlike the athame, a boline is a working tool. Some uses are harvesting herbs and carving words onto candles.

INSTANT WITCH TIP – Blades

The athame and boline do not need to be a specific colour or shape. The point (ha ha) is that the athame is used for directing energy and the boline is used for physically cutting.

SCISSORS

A combination of two blades fastened together. While the athame and boline are more traditional, the functionality of scissors can't be beat. Keep a special pair of sharp scissors that you only use for magickal purposes.

INSTANT WITCH TIP – Safety first

Before using sharp tools, pause for a second and thank the blade. Take a moment to focus before cutting and save yourself an inconvenient ER trip (been there).

✳ WAND ✳

Another iconic tool, a wand is used to direct energy, similar to an athame. Usually they are made of wood, but I've seen some beautiful crystal wands. They are associated with either the fire or air elements. And they are considered masculine because … well, you've seen a wand. A wand serves to focus energy to a specific point. You can use your wand to draw words in the air or even to activate magickal crafts, such as sigils or symbols, by pointing it at them.

✳ BROOM ✳

Witches don't just use brooms to fly on. They are a powerful tool for purification and cleansing. A ubiquitous household staple, few items have more superstitions around them than brooms.

- To get an unwanted guest to leave, flip your broom upside down. (If they still won't leave, flip your broom upside down and point them to this page.)
- Hang a broom above your front door for protection. It is said evil spirits cannot cross brooms.
- In the Southern United States, it is said sweeping after dusk will bring bad luck.
- Some believe if someone sweeps over your feet, you won't get married. If that happens, spit on the broom to avoid misfortune.

✷ CRYSTALS ✷

It's easy to be captivated by the beauty and energy of crystals. Crystals are like magickal batteries that can be used and drawn upon for different purposes. Crystals come from the ground and are associated with the earth element. Each crystal has traditional qualities, so select appropriate crystals for the task. For example, pyrite, with its gold colour, is normally used in financial workings. In a pinch, clear quartz is a good 'catch-all' crystal. Having said that, be guided by the crystals you are drawn to – trust your instincts.

Using crystals	Meditate while holding a crystal.
	Place a crystal an altar (pages 116–117).
	Add a crystal to a spell jar.
	Arrange crystals around a ritual circle (page 129).

✷ BOOK OF SHADOWS ✷

A place for you to write your magickal findings, this can be a physical notebook, or you can use an electronic medium, such as a Google Doc. Your book of shadows might contain spells, recipes and correspondences.

✷ GRIMOIRE ✷

A collection of spells, rituals and instructions. The difference between a book of shadows and a grimoire is that a book of shadows is for personal use and a grimoire is meant to be passed down or used in a group.

✷ THE FARMER'S ALMANAC ✷

This is the first reference I recommend for beginner witches. Almanacs are jam-packed with folk remedies, astrological transits, phases of the Moon and planting days: everything a farmer could need. Farmers and witches have a remarkable amount in common.

ASTROLOGY

ASTROLOGY

THE NATURAL CYCLES OF THE HEAVENS

WITCHCRAFT IS BASED on the natural cycles of the universe, which we can recognize running through astrology, the phases of the Moon and the wheel of the year. Is your fate written in the stars? In this section, we will cover the basics of astrology. You will learn about the zodiac, planets and natal chart basics.

Astrology is an ancient science, only recently watered down into what we know as horoscopes. I could fill 100 pages on astrology and barely scratch the surface. It's essentially space maths. Alas, I am breezing over a few things here (sorry, houses!) but this should be enough to get you started. And if all this does is whet your curiosity – great! Dive into the limitless study of the heavens.

INSTANT WITCH TIP – You have been warned

If you learn astrology, you will be asked to read your friends' birth charts. Congratulations. You're now the 'I have a friend who can …' friend. It's a cool party trick and conversation-starter, but don't say I didn't warn you...

What is Astrology?

Astrology, in a nutshell, is the study of patterns, an ancient practice that explores the movement of heavenly bodies and human behaviour. As convenient as it would be, astrology is not set in stone. You cannot predict the winning lottery numbers using astrology. You could determine an extra lucky day to buy a ticket, though, because it identifies the prevailing energies so that you can work with them, not against them.

Each of the 12 zodiac signs is assigned a 30-degree 'slice' of the sky as we look up from Earth. This is what it means when people say the Sun is 'in' Aries, for example. All 12 signs of the zodiac are associated with different energetic archetypes.

If someone tells you they are a Taurus, they mean that the Sun was transiting through the 30-degree section of sky associated with Taurus when they were born. The Sun 'transits' through each zodiac sign in a bit longer than 30 days. Think about it. There are 360 degrees in a circle and 365.25 days in a year. No, the Sun is not actually moving – but that is how it appears from the Earth.

WITCHY KNOWLEDGE - Astrological systems

There are several different systems used in astrology. I am a Westerner (Virginia, USA, born and raised) and use the Western system of astrology.

Modality

Before we look in a bit more depth at the 12 zodiac signs with which you are all familiar, you need to understand that every zodiac sign aligns with one of three modalities: cardinal, fixed or mutable. These relate to where a sign falls within its season: the beginning, middle or end. No signs from the same element have the same modality, so there is only one cardinal air sign (Libra), for example. Each zodiac sign has a unique combination of its element and modality that affects the predominant energies.

CARDINAL SIGNS

- Aries, Libra, Cancer, Capricorn.
- The first sign of its season.
- Initiators and action-takers.
- Starting brand new projects and endeavours.

MUTABLE SIGNS

- Gemini, Sagittarius, Virgo, Pisces.
- The last sign in its season.
- Flexible and adaptable.
- Wrapping up and transitioning into the next season.

FIXED SIGNS

- Taurus, Scorpio, Leo, Aquarius.
- The middle sign in its season.
- Stubborn and unyielding.
- Continuing the work begun by the previous sign.

THE 12 SIGNS OF THE ZODIAC

THE 12 ZODIAC signs are the basis of astrology. Below are the energetic archetypes of each sign. We all have all 12 archetypal energies within us, regardless of whether a certain sign appears in our birth charts, but they vary in strength.

The dates of each Sun season vary by a day or two each year. If you're on the cusp, Google it or consult *The Farmer's Almanac*.

ARIES *21 March–19 April*

Baby Aries is the first sign of the zodiac. Symbolized by the ram, Aries is a natural-born leader. Aries is a cardinal fire sign, ruled by the planet Mars. The start of Aries season coincides with the vernal equinox, and beginning of spring in the northern hemisphere. Shadows of Aries include selfishness, impulsiveness and competitiveness.

TAURUS *20 April–20 May*

Indulgent Taurus is the second sign of the zodiac. Symbolized by the bull, Taurus lives in the material world. Taurus is a fixed earth sign, ruled by the planet Venus. Shadows of Taurus include materialism, stubbornness and unwillingness to leave their comfort zone.

GEMINI *21 May–20 June*

Inquisitive Gemini is the third sign of the zodiac. Symbolized by the twins, Castor and Pollux, Gemini embraces duality. Gemini is a mutable air sign, ruled by the planet Mercury. Shadows of Gemini include ungroundedness, volatile emotions and commitment issues.

CANCER *21 June–22 July*

Maternal Cancer is the fourth sign of the zodiac. Symbolized by the crab, Cancer carries their home with them. Cancer is a cardinal water sign, ruled by the Moon. The start of Cancer season coincides with the summer solstice and beginning of summer in the northern hemisphere. Shadows of Cancer include passive-aggressiveness, moodiness and control issues.

LEO *23 July–22 August*

Proud Leo is the fifth sign of the zodiac. Symbolized by the Lion, Leos are not afraid to roar. Leo is a fixed fire sign, ruled by the Sun. Shadows of Leo include attention-seeking behaviour, narcissism and pride.

VIRGO *23 August–22 September*

Pure Virgo is the sixth sign of the zodiac. Symbolized by the Virgin, Virgo craves perfection. Virgo is a mutable earth sign, ruled by Mercury. Shadows of Virgo include perfectionism, nit-picking, and self-doubt.

LIBRA *23 September–22 October*

Aesthetic Libra is the seventh sign of the zodiac. Symbolized by the scales, Libra is the only sign represented by an inanimate object. Libra is a cardinal air sign, ruled by Venus. The start of Libra season coincides with the autumn equinox and the beginning of fall or autumn in the northern hemisphere. Shadows of Libra include indecisiveness, flakiness and shallowness.

SCORPIO *23 October– 21 November*

Transformative Scorpio is the eighth sign of the zodiac. Symbolized by the Scorpion, Scorpio is not afraid to sting. Scorpio is a fixed water sign, traditionally ruled by Mars. Modern astrologists associate Pluto with Scorpio. Shadows of Scorpio include holding grudges, guardedness and mistrustfulness.

SAGITTARIUS *22 November–21 December*

Adventurous Sagittarius is the ninth sign of the zodiac. Symbolized by the archer, Sagittarius is ready for a journey. Sagittarius is a mutable fire sign, ruled by Jupiter. Shadows of Sagittarius include 'know-it-all' energy, irresponsibility and overindulgence.

CAPRICORN *22 December–19 January*

Symbolized by the sea goat, disciplined Capricorn is the tenth sign of the zodiac. Capricorn is a cardinal earth sign, ruled by Saturn. The start of Capricorn season coincides with the winter solstice and the beginning of winter in the northern hemisphere. Shadows of Capricorn include pessimism, workaholism and greed.

AQUARIUS *20 January–18 February*

Innovative Aquarius is the eleventh and penultimate sign of the zodiac. Symbolized by the water-bearer, Aquarius yearns to spread knowledge. Aquarius is a fixed air sign (not a water sign, even though it is the water-carrier), ruled by Saturn. Shadows of Aquarius include condescension, rebelliousness and detachment.

PISCES *19 February–20 March*

Mystical Pisces is the twelfth and final sign of the zodiac. Symbolized by the fish, Pisces is a highly spiritual sign. Pisces is a mutable water sign, ruled by the Moon. Shadows of Pisces include escapism, boundary issues and a victim mindset.

OTHER INFLUENCERS

While Sun signs take priority, there are other factors that influence the energies around us and have a bearing on our charts.

✷ PLANETS ✷

In astrology, the Sun and Moon are considered planets, even though technically they are a star and, well, a moon.

I find it helpful to view the planets as people. These 'people' take on different personalities, depending on what zodiac sign they are in. The Sun in Aries behaves differently from the Sun in Libra. Within your birth chart, these 'people' interact with each other.

Sun	The centre of the solar system, the Sun is associated with our sense of self, and linked to our overall personality.
Moon	The Earth's closest celestial body. The Moon is associated with our emotions, intuition and subconscious, and is so important it has its own chapter in this book (pages 54–71).
Mercury	Mercury, the messenger planet, is associated with communication and technology.
Venus	Venus, the planet of love and beauty, is associated with relationships, romance and aesthetics.

Mars	Mars, the planet of action, is associated with passion, war and aggression.
Jupiter	Jupiter, the planet of good fortune, is associated with expansion, prosperity and luck.
Saturn	Saturn, the planet of authority, is associated with discipline and boundaries. Big daddy energy.
Uranus	Uranus, the great awakener, is associated with rebellion and dramatic change.
Neptune	Neptune, the planet of illusions and dreams, is associated with imagination and intuition.
Pluto	In astrology (and our hearts) Pluto is considered a planet. The furthest planet from Earth, Pluto is associated with death and rebirth.

✷ WEEKLY WITCHCRAFT ✷

Each day of the week has its own planetary ruler and associated colour. Try structuring your tasks taking into account the energy of each day. For a little glamour magic, wear the planet's associated colour.

Sunday	Sun	Yellow
Monday	Moon	White
Tuesday	Mars	Red
Wednesday	Mercury	Blue
Thursday	Jupiter	Green
Friday	Venus	Pink
Saturday	Saturn	Black

✷ ASPECTS ✷

Aspects are the angles between celestial bodies, and can help us understand how they are influencing each other. The major classical aspects are conjunction, opposition, square, trine and sextile.

CONJUNCTION

Conjunctions occur when planets are in the same sign, within 8 degrees of each other. When conjunct, planets amplify each other's energy. New moons always occur when the Sun and Moon are conjunct.

OPPOSITION

Oppositions occur when planets are, well, opposite each other: a full 180 degrees apart on an astrological chart. Oppositions are considered challenging aspects, as they indicate an astrological push-pull between two energies. Full moons are always opposition aspects.

TRINE

Trines occur when planets are 120 degrees from each other.
They are considered harmonious.

SQUARE

Squares occur when planets are 90 degrees from each other.
They can indicate friction or tension.

SEXTILE

Sextiles occur when planets are 60 degrees from each other.
They are considered positive.

✷ RETROGRADES ✷

Retrogrades get a bad rap. Retrogrades occur when planets appear to move backwards in the sky, due to the Earth passing a slower-moving planet. This is an optical illusion, similar to when you are in a stationary car and the car next to you pulls forward. It feels like you're going backwards, but really, you stayed in the same place. Retrogrades turn the energy of the planets inward.

The correct terminology is that a planet *is* retrograde, not *in* retrograde. There is no portion of the sky called 'retrograde'. Technically, 'in apparent retrograde motion', would be most accurate, but doesn't that sound snooty?

When you think of retrogrades, think 're'. Revisiting. Redoing. Reworking. REEE. Kidding. Retrogrades teach us that, sometimes, to go forward, you must go back.

MERCURY RETROGRADE

The most notorious of retrogrades is Mercury. Mercury in the microwave. Due to Mercury's association with technology and communication, this retrograde is felt strongly in day-to-day life. Flights cancelled. Websites down. Meetings missed. There are some clears dos and don'ts when Mercury is retrograde.

Do:

- Journal.
- Back up your work – save frequently.
- Overcommunicate.
- Take any electronic errors as time to makes space for nature.
- Finish old projects.
- Be careful and intentional with electronics.
- Replace that broken phone screen.
- Expect workplace conflict.
- Set emails to send five minutes in the future.

Don't:

- Start any new work or projects.
- Sign any contracts.
- Get back together with your ex.

Plotting & Reading Your Natal Chart

You can download natal charts and fill them in manually or have one done for you. My favourite website for birth charts is Café Astrology (astro.cafeastrology.com). Basically, a natal chart will show you a map of the heavens at the time you were born. Once you have plotted all the celestial bodies, you can interpret them one at a time, gradually adding to and refining the unique picture as you go.

✷ THE BIG THREE ✷

If you pull your birth chart and are overwhelmed by lines and symbols, don't panic. Start by learning your 'big three': your Sun, Moon and rising signs. The Sun and Moon are both considered luminaries, meaning they are the brightest sources of light in the sky.

SUN SIGN

Almost everyone knows their Sun sign, which relates to the position of the Sun when a person was born. Your sun sign shows the overall expression of your personality and how you shine.

MOON SIGN

The position of the Moon when you were born defines your emotional temperament.

RISING SIGN

The rising sign, or ascendant, is the constellation appearing on the eastern horizon (where the Sun rises) when you were born. The rising sign begins with your first house (sadly, houses are beyond the scope of this book), and is how you appear to others outwardly. To calculate your rising sign, you need your exact birth time (the ascendant changes every few minutes). This information can be found on your birth certificate, or you may need to call your mum. If that's not possible, pull astrology charts at several different times on the day you were born. If you can't figure it out, that's okay too – people lead happy lives without ever knowing their rising sign.

SHADOW WORK

THE SHADOW SELF is a concept popularized by the psychiatrist Carl Jung. It indicates unresolved problems. Shadows are largely formed before we can consciously control them, during those impressionable infant years. Ever get yelled at for being too loud, or expressing yourself differently? These wounds can impact your behaviour years later. They can also be used for self-improvement. This journey isn't linear, and is uncomfortable at times. Shadow work can be painful, but healing. Through introspection, we can work through old traumas and become the best versions of ourselves.

One thing you take on when starting witchcraft is the never-ending struggle with the shadow self, the ceaseless drive to self-improve and heal any wounds that need healing. As we transit through each zodiac sign, check in with yourself and determine if you can 'tune in' to the optimal energy of each sign. At the same time, what zodiac sign the Moon is in, and see if you are aligning with the shadows of that sign. The best times for shadow work are during the full or dark moons.

Shadow work journalling questions

Follow the full moon ritual (page 60), answering these questions in your journal.

- **What traits do you see in your parents that annoy you?** Do you see them within yourself?
- **Describe an emotional childhood memory.** What emotion did you feel? What advice would you give to a child experiencing those feelings?
- **Describe a time you made a mistake.** How did you resolve it? What did you learn from it?
- **How did your parents treat you when you made a mistake?**

✷ PARENTAL WOUNDS ✷

There's no such thing as a perfect parent – after all, we are only human and we all get frazzled and lose our tempers now and again. Most of us are fortunate enough to get over such incidents: when your dad, annoyed, told you to keep quiet when singing; when your mum, frazzled, yelled at you for breaking a glass. We learn the lesson and try to avoid repeating it, without it impacting us negatively.

Some people, however, find that their mother or father wounds from childhood remain unhealed. Parents do not need to be abusive to create these wounds. Wounds can stem from a single traumatic interaction. It is likely that these wounds have come from unhealed wounds in your mother and father that were passed down from their mother and father. Acknowledging and healing these wounds is a core part of shadow work. Otherwise, the cycle of these wounds will continue to haunt you.

Exercise to heal a parental wound
This is a simple but powerful spell to clear a traumatic incident.

You will need: A white candle.

- Light a white candle.
- Picture a negative scenario from your childhood involving your mother and father.
- Gently parent yourself through the situation. Would you have reacted differently?
- Forgive yourself and them (unless they were abusive, in which case, fuck 'em).

Using astrology and energetic archetypes, we can work to heal old wounds. As a witch, feel empowered to look inward, and know you have the tools to mend anything that comes up. When your shadows are triggered, write in your journal, take a ritual bath, or even give your familiar a good pet. Shadow work can be emotionally intense – give yourself grace and don't try to work on every shadow at once. Just by becoming aware of these shadows, we can learn to overcome them.

The Moon

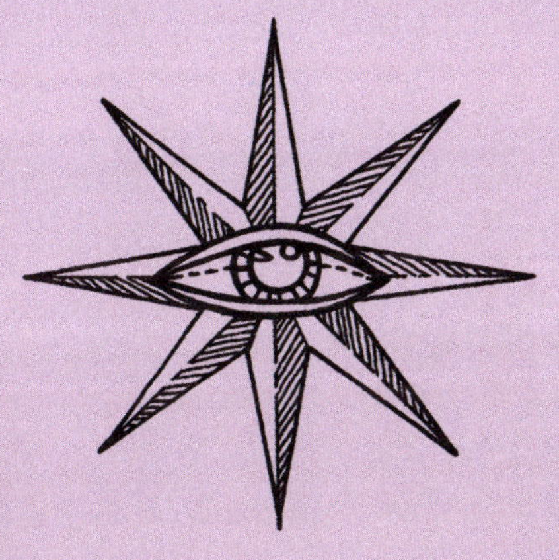

The Lunar Cycle

Hello, neighbour Moon. The Moon is the closest celestial body to the Earth. Her effect on humanity is impossible to ignore. If you know any ER nurses, they will tell you how crazy things get during the full moon. The Moon's journey through the month is another powerful cycle to work with on your journey into witchcraft. Even those uninterested in astrology have had their breath taken away by a particularly stunning full moon.

Wolves howl at the Moon. Witches dance naked under the full moon (allegedly). We know scientifically that the Moon affects water in the form of high and low tides. Humans are made up of roughly 70% water – therefore it comes as no surprise that the Moon impacts behaviour. When we keep track of the Moon's cycle, we work with her power. And yes, the Moon's a she – at least in my practice. Technically, she's a large genderless rock. But for witchy purposes, the Moon is closely linked to our emotions and the divine feminine. In both Greek and Roman mythology, the moon goddess is a woman (Selene and Luna, respectively). Use an ephemeris or witchy calendar to keep track of the phases of the Moon.

A full lunar cycle, sometimes called a lunar month, lasts 29.5 days. It begins and ends at each respective new moon. The full moon is the peak of the lunar cycle. When the Moon is waxing, it is growing in light. When it is waning, the Moon's appearance shrinks. Lunation is a fancy name for the amount of time occurring between two new moons.

✳ PHASES OF THE MOON ✳

The Moon itself never changes shape (in case that's not obvious!). Regardless of whether the Moon is new or full, it remains a giant sphere. The lunar phases are the current *apparent* shape of the Moon, as in, how much of the Moon we see from Earth due to the reflection of sunlight on the Moon's surface.

The phases of the moon are caused by its relative position to the Earth and the Sun. Depending on its position, the Moon reflects a certain amount of sunlight: during the new moon, it reflects no light, and during the full moon, it is fully illuminated.

The Moon's cycle is one of life, death and subsequent rebirth, and every lunar phase carries a different, equally important energy. For witchy purposes, these energies are grouped into four different types: new, waxing, full and waning.

WITCHY KNOWLEDGE - Astronomical Moon

If we're talking astronomy, the Moon has eight different phases: new moon, waxing crescent, first quarter, waxing gibbous, full moon, waning gibbous, third quarter and waning crescent.

NEW MOON

The new moon is the first phase of the lunar cycle, the equivalent to a woman's menstrual phase. New moons occur when the Moon is between the Earth and the Sun. It is a time of new beginnings and introspection, when the Moon is dark in the sky. During the new moon, plant seeds to nurture during the cycle ahead.

New moons always occur in the same zodiac sign as the current Sun sign. The new moon in Aquarius will always occur during Aquarius season.

WAXING MOON

This includes the waxing crescent, first quarter and waxing gibbous.

The waxing moon is a time of increase and build-up. The light of the Moon begins to grow but is not yet at its full power. This is equivalent to a woman's follicular phase, where she typically feels happier, productive and more energized.

FULL MOON

The full moon is the peak of the lunar cycle, when the Moon is fully illuminated in the sky, the equivalent to a woman's ovulatory phase. The Moon's full light reveals our shadows and highlights our gifts. The full moon is the perfect time for most spellwork (except for manifesting new beginnings – that's best saved for under the new moon).

Full moons occur when the Moon opposes the Sun with the Earth in the middle. They also always occur in the opposing zodiac to the current Sun sign. There are only full moons in Gemini during Sagittarius season, and vice versa. There can never be a full moon in Aries during Taurus season.

WANING MOON

This includes the waning gibbous, third quarter and waning crescent.

The waning moon is a time of decrease and reflection. The Moon begins to shrink as it returns to darkness. This is equivalent to a woman's luteal phase, where she starts to wind down. Moods and energy levels are low, and it may feel difficult to get shit done.

DARK MOON

The period of waning right before the new moon begins the next lunar cycle, when the Moon appears fully black but is not yet renewed. The death of the current cycle.

✷ HOW TO DO A FULL MOON RITUAL ✷

Another common phrase – but what is a full moon ritual, really? A ritual is a set of actions performed in sequence with intention. The most boring everyday activities can be turned into powerful rituals with a little thought. The bright full moon is a popular time for magickal rituals.

Full moon journalling ritual

This is how I do my ritual. If anything else speaks to you, feel free to add it.

You will need: Your journal, crystals and candles.

- First, decide if you want to do the ritual solo or with a group.
- Gather any supplies.
- Before starting, I like to do a few minutes of yoga to connect with my body.
- Meditate for five to ten minutes.
- When you feel centred, take out your journal and answer these questions.
    - What energy am I leaving in the past?
    - How do I want to feel by the next full moon?
    - Who drained my energy this month?
    - Are there any energetic ties I need to release?
    - Did I encounter any blockages this month?
- When that feels complete, take a ritual bath (page 101).

New moon journalling questions

You can do a similar exercise at the new moon, answering the following questions.

- What am I beginning this month?
- What am I removing from my to-do list?
- How will I recharge myself this month?
- What is my top goal for this month?
- What pattern am I focusing on shifting?

✷ FULL MOON NAMES ✷

Every full moon has a name. Learning what each full moon is called helps understand its energy, and how it fits into each season. The names for each full moon come from Native American, Colonial American and European traditions.

If you are in the southern hemisphere, these moons will occur in the opposite months of the year, so the Wolf Moon occurs in July, the Snow Moon in August, and so on.

Wolf Moon	January	When wolves can be heard howling.
Snow Moon	February	When snow is often on the ground.
Worm Moon	March	When worms begin to emerge from their nests.
Pink Moon	April	When the first pink flowers bloom.
Flower Moon	May	When flowers grow abundantly.
Strawberry Moon	June	When strawberries appear.
Buck Moon	July	When bucks' antlers mature.
Sturgeon Moon	August	When fish are plentiful and easily caught.
Corn/Harvest Moon	September	When corn is traditionally harvested.
Hunter Moon	October	When game is hunted to prepare for winter.
Beaver Moon	November	When beavers retreat into their dens.
Cold Moon	December	When the winter's chill is felt.

How to Manifest with the Moon

Contrary to popular belief, the best time for manifesting is not the full moon – it's the new moon. New moons, as they begin the lunar cycle, offer a fresh start. New moons are restful times when there is less light in the sky, so they are the perfect time for journalling, meditating and filling out your planner.

The waxing moon is when to take inspired action. It's a time of growth, when there is more light and energy to be used. During the waxing moon, do the dang thing. Take steps towards what you planned to manifest during the new moon.

Full moons, when the Moon is at its brightest, are a time of heightened energy. Schedule any activities that require a lot of juice around the full moon. Full moons are a highlight and subsequent release.

The waning moon is when to reflect on the month so far: what's going well, what's not working out, and what you can adjust for the next cycle? Are there any final edits or changes that can be made?

Wait until the new moon is here before starting any new manifestations. The dark moon, the period right before the new moon while the moon is still waning, is a time of shadow work and death – not exactly the best time to start something new.

INSTANT WITCH TIP – Choosing your Moon energy

Workings to manifest or increase are best done when the Moon is new or waxing. Workings to release or decrease are best done when the Moon is full to waning.

Moon-gazing meditation
This is a simple meditation exercise.

- Go somewhere you can see the Moon – ideally outside, but inside works as well. If this is simply not possible, draw or print out a picture of the Moon and place it in front of you.
- Ensure the area is free of distractions. Lock out any pets or nosy roommates. Close your eyes if that feels comfortable; if not, soften your gaze.
- Take three deep breaths. Imagine the stress of the day coming off you in waves.
- When you feel relaxed, open your eyes and look at the Moon. Focus solely on the Moon and try to clear your mind. Attune your vibration to the energy of the Moon. Allow yourself to receive any messages coming to you. It might sound like your inner voice, or coming to a sudden realization.
- Ask any questions you need answered. Speak them aloud, if possible; use your inner voice if not. Keep an open mind to any thoughts, people or situations that pop up.
- When the meditation feels complete, thank the Moon. Write down any findings in your journal.

FULL MOONS, WHEN THE MOON IS AT ITS BRIGHTEST, ARE A TIME OF HEIGHTENED ENERGY.

Charging under the Moon

The Moon's light holds powerful energy. Witches can harness this power by cleansing and charging items under the Moon. To charge an item, place it somewhere directly in the Moon's light. Outside is best, but in a window also works. Leave it there overnight and do your best to collect it before the Sun touches it. If the Sun does, that's okay – it will just also be infused with the Sun's energy.

Crystals work like magickal batteries and hold the Moon's charge wonderfully. Check the weather forecast before charging crystals outside. Most crystals that end in 'ite' are water soluble, so start to dissolve when wet.

Get creative with what you charge under the Moon. It doesn't just have to be magickal items. Charge your hairbrush, candles, a jar of pickles – the sky's the limit (pun intended).

✷ MOONWATER ✷

For a double energetic whammy, you can make moonwater. Moonwater is basically charged water. Water, at a molecular level, can absorb vibrations and energies.

Making moonwater is as simple as leaving water out underneath the Moon. It is most commonly made under the full moon. However, it can be made during any phase. For a fresh start, try making water under the new moon in your Sun or rising zodiac sign.

All you need to make moonwater is water and a container: old jars, wine bottles – anything clear. Glass works best; it is debatable if the Moon's energy penetrates plastic. Personally, I use plastic, but I've been roasted for it online, so your mileage may vary. Chaos-inclined witches may even throw a pack of bottled water outside and call it a day.

First, decide on an intention for your moonwater. Do you want it to do anything specific, or do you just wish to capture a bit of full moon energy? With your intention in mind, cleanse your container normally. Then, spiritually cleanse it (pages 97–101) with your tool of choice (incense, smoke bundle, singing bowl or whatever). When it's good and cleansed, add water, all the while focusing on that intention. Place the container of water outside or by a window where it is under the Moon's light. Collect your moonwater in the morning. Wherever you would use normal water, you can substitute moonwater for some extra magick.

There are many ways to use moonwater.

- Drink it.
- Water your plants.
- Cleanse magickal tools.
- Add to a ritual bath (page 101).
- Make tea.

✷ VOID-OF-COURSE MOONS ✷

The Moon becomes void-of-course when it makes the last major aspect before it changes from one sign of the zodiac to the next. The void of-course period ends when the Moon enters the next sign.

The Moon rules our inner, emotional world. When the Moon is void, she is off on her own, without any influence from any other planets. Void-of-course moons can cause us to feel unproductive, distracted or overtly dreamy. The Moon doesn't have retrograde periods as other planets do (page 49), but some astrologers consider the energy of a void-of-course Moon similar to a retrograde.

Avoid buying anything when the Moon is void-of-course. Purchases will be ill-used or returned. Typically, void-of-course periods are short, lasting a few minutes to a few hours. When there is a long void period, I suggest marking it in your calendar.

During a void-of-course moon, do:

- Submit things you don't want a result from, such as sending an email where you don't want a reply.
- Imagine a 'void' stamp on any activities started during a void-of-course moon.
- Meditate.
- Journal.
- Wrap up any projects.
- Lean in to daydreams and creativity.

During a void-of-course moon, don't:

- Start new activities.
- Sign any contracts.
- Buy anything – unless it's routine.
- Force productivity.

OTHER CYCLICAL EVENTS

There are other celestial events that we take into consideration.

ECLIPSES

As it appears from Earth, the Sun and Moon dance around the sky. Twice a year, these two star-crossed lovers meet in a shadowy embrace, known as an eclipse. Civilizations, such as the Maya, have been observing and worshiping eclipses for thousands of years.

Eclipses occur when a celestial body blocks the Sun's light, casting a shadow. They happen in pairs of one solar and one lunar eclipse, twice a year. The time between a pair of eclipses is known as eclipse season.

The period between eclipse seasons can feel like filler episodes, with the time during eclipse season containing the dramatic events of the year. Eclipses occur in the same pair of opposing zodiac signs for approximately 18 months before moving into the next pair of signs. When an eclipse occurs in one of your big three zodiac signs (Sun, moon and rising), or a sign in which you have a stellium (three or more planets in the same sign), buckle up. The energies of both signs involved in the eclipse will be amplified – both the highs and the lows. Eclipses, similar to retrograde, invite us to go with the flow. While travelling during eclipse season, my car broke down out of nowhere (and on a Sunday...). No mechanics were open – it was a whole thing. Around eclipses, expect random, chaotic events to test your patience.

On mother Earth, we observe two types of eclipse: lunar and solar.

LUNAR ECLIPSE

Lunar eclipses occur during special full moons, when the Moon moves into Earth's shadow. This can cause the Moon to be dimmed, or even appear red. This denotes an intense, often uncontrollable time of transformation and destruction.

SOLAR ECLIPSE

Solar eclipses occur during powerful new moons. During a solar eclipse, the Moon moves between the Sun and Earth, blocking the Sun's light. During total eclipses, the Moon completely covers the Sun. This can cause the eerie effect of darkness during the day. If you are lucky enough to witness one, it is profound experience – the birds stop singing, and the stillness and darkness in the day seem to have a spiritual dimension. Solar eclipses often usher in a new chapter of life.

✷ WORKING WITH ECLIPSES ✷

Among the witch community, there is debate around the efficacy of working with eclipses. Some consider eclipses something to be survived. Others, especially those of the chaos magick school of thought, embrace eclipses for their destructive energy. Spellwork during eclipses is akin to lighting a match with wildfire. I recommend intentionally experiencing one eclipse season before trying to harness its power.

Eclipse journalling questions
Look up the next solar and lunar eclipse and mark the dates in your calendar.

- When the eclipse is exact, go outside and answer these questions in your journal.
  - How do you feel?
  - Have any major events happened recently?
  - Are there any areas in your life in which you have experienced a dramatic beginning or ending?

The Menstrual Cycle

Can you think of another cycle that lasts roughly 29.5 days? If you've experienced one, it's a no-brainer – a menstrual cycle. Bleeding, while inconvenient, lets us know it is a time to rest and recharge. Capitalism encourages us to live on a 24-hour clock of five days on and two days off. For many, especially those with a menstrual cycle, this is not realistic. Women's hormones, like the Moon, fluctuate on a monthly basis.

Keep track of the lunar phase in which you menstruate. You might see a pattern. My cycle is slightly longer than average, and alternates between a red and white cycle. When we become aware of the natural cycle within us, we can work with it and not against it.

RED MOON CYCLE

If you menstruate on the full moon, you are on a red moon cycle. This cycle goes against modern feminine stereotypes. It's about dark feminine energy; the wise woman archetype; the witch. Your body wants to go inward while the full moon urges you to go outward. Take this period as a time of introspection and magick. Do a full moon ritual. Light that candle you've been saving. Finish those half-finished crafts. While others may urge you to go out, stay home and focus your energy inward.

WHITE MOON CYCLE

If you menstruate on the new moon, you are on a white moon cycle. This is the most 'normal' cycle to be on. The menstruation period and new moon go hand in hand, energetically. New moons are naturally a time of rest. It's about feminine energy, the mother archetype. Your body is calling your energy inward, while the Moon is also calling you inward. Take this period as a time of rest and planning. Journal, meditate, take an everything shower. Turn into a prune in a ritual bath (page 101). This is your friendly reminder that rest is productive, despite what capitalism wants us to think.

Menstrual blood, called moon blood, is an extremely powerful taglock (page 140). It's blood, but it comes directly from the womb, the giver of life. In folklore, it is said that if you feed a lover your moon blood, they will be devoted to you forever. I cannot recommend feeding someone your blood without their consent. But if you wanted to carve their name on a red candle and anoint it with your moon blood, I certainly couldn't stop you. Be careful with this one, though – only do it on someone you are serious with. Or ignore me, but don't say I didn't warn you.

THIS IS YOUR FRIENDLY REMINDER THAT REST IS PRODUCTIVE, DESPITE WHAT CAPITALISM WANTS US TO THINK.

THE WHEEL OF THE YEAR

SAMAIN
OCT 31
YULE
DEC 20–23
WINTER SOLSTICE
IMBOLC
FEB 2
OSTARA
MAR 20–23
SPRING EQUINOX
BELTANE
MAY 1
LITHA
JUN 20–23
SUMMER SOLSTICE
LUGHNASADH
AUG 1
MABON
SEPT 20–23
AUTUMN EQUINOX

The Modern Pagan Wheel

The wheel of the year is a modern pagan system of holidays aligned with the seasons. In this section, you'll gain an understanding of the spirit of each celebration and learn how to coordinate your practice with the natural energies of the world.

Not all witches are pagan, and not all pagans are witches. Following the wheel of the year is not a requirement. Still, developing an understanding of these energies will help you connect with your local environment. Harmonizing with the natural cycle of the seasons enhances your inner power and connection to the Earth. It's easy to start a new project in spring, and nigh impossible to start planting in the dead of winter.

Frankly, it is shocking to me that everyone doesn't celebrate the wheel of the year. Who doesn't want eight equally spaced holidays? And they're all synchronized with the seasons. Sign me up.

✳ THE SABBATS ✳

The wheel of the year is a modern calendar of pagan festivals. It consists of eight pagan holidays, called sabbats. These sabbats (pronounced 'sab-uht') make up the spokes of the wheel. They are equally spaced and line up with seasonal energies.

As Friedrich Nietzsche once said, time is a flat circle. The wheel of the year represents the eternal turn of time, never ending, always turning – whether we're ready or not. Use these holidays to honour the season that has passed and prepare for the weather ahead.

Our planet travels through space in an elliptical pattern around the Sun. Depending on where the Earth is in its orbit, we experience the seasons.

The Earth is not straight in relation to the Sun – it tilts at 23.5 degrees. This tilt causes different areas of the planet to receive varying amounts of the Sun's energy throughout the year.

The Earth's axial tilt is the reason the sabbats differ in the northern and southern hemispheres. Essentially, the celebrations are flipped. Those in the northern hemisphere celebrate the winter solstice while those in the southern celebrate the summer solstice, and so on. Dates for the sabbats in both hemispheres are noted later in this chapter.

Four of the festivals – Imbolc, Beltane, Lughnasadh and Samhain – are traditional Celtic fire festivals. These are known as the cross-quarter days, as they fall in the middle of the solstices and equinoxes.

The other four – the spring equinox, summer solstice, autumn equinox and winter solstice – are connected to the changing of the seasons: spring, summer, autumn (or fall) and winter, respectively (in case that's not obvious).

The sabbats, when considered together, tell a story of the seasons. They honour the death of winter, the rebirth of spring, the vitality of summer and the bounty of autumn (fall).

Each festival venerates a shift within nature: the ebb and flow of light and dark. The wheel begins with the darkness of Yule and ends with the witch's new year, Samhain.

Feel free to celebrate the sabbats on days that align with your local weather and harvesting season. As a witch, it is important to connect with the spirit of the land around you. For each sabbat, spend time outside in nature. Whether that is simply going for a walk or doing a more involved meditation is up to you. Don't forget to bundle up for the colder sabbats. Many witches opt to celebrate the warmer sabbats in the nude.

I find it helpful to time any energetic protections and deep cleanses with the solstices and equinoxes. This spaces them evenly throughout the year and makes it easy to keep track of what needs done.

INSTANT WITCH TIP – Make your own wheel

Try displaying a physical representation of the wheel of the year as one would a normal 12-month calendar. Buy or create your own wheel, and turn it as the seasons change. There even are wooden wheels available that you can paint yourself.

Don't feel pressured to go all out for every holiday. Not all witches celebrate all (or any) sabbats. Pick the ones that align with you and go from there. The society you live in probably already celebrates a few of these. Many contemporary holidays are co-opted from pagan celebrations (thanks, Christianity).

✷ EQUINOX ✷

Derived from the Latin word *aequinoctium* – a combination of *aequus*, meaning equal, and *nox*, meaning night. On the two annual equinoxes, day and night are of approximately equal length. After each equinox, the balance shifts, with days growing in either darkness or light.

✷ SOLSTICE ✷

Derived from the Latin words *sol*, meaning sun, and *sistere*, meaning to stand still, the two annual solstices are times of maximum light and dark. The longest day is the summer solstice, and the longest night is the winter solstice.

WICCA & THE WHEEL OF THE YEAR

No single group historically celebrated all these holidays. The wheel of the year is a Wiccan amalgam of appropriated cultural traditions, popularized in the mid-1900s by Gerald Gardner and Ross Nichols.

Gerald Gardner is known as the 'father of Wicca'. He wrote prolifically on high magick and witchcraft. Ross Nichols is credited with reviving interest in Celtic neopaganism and Druidry. Most notably, he founded the Order of Bards, Ovates and Druids in 1964.

Aidan Kelly, another prominent figure in Wicca, named the summer solstice and spring and autumn equinox holidays (Litha, Ostara and Mabon respectively) in 1974. In the context of history, this very recent.

Wicca and witchcraft are not one and the same. The Venn diagram of Wiccas and witches has a lot of overlap, sure. But not every Wiccan is a witch. Wicca is an Earth-based religion that embraces magick. Their mythos centres around the divine feminine and masculine: the Goddess and the Horned God, respectively. Like the wheel of the year, Wicca is relatively new in origin.

Personally, I don't consider myself Wiccan. There are too many rules, and some of the founders were a tad problematic. I encourage you to be wary of any spiritual groups founded and run primarily by men. But if you come from a background of organized religion, you might find comfort in the ceremonial aspect of Wicca.

I am sharing the Wiccan lore here because it can be a helpful metaphor for understanding the energy of each of the sabbats. Wiccan mythology tells a story of death, love and rebirth.

WITCHY KNOWLEDGE - The sabbats

I want to reiterate that the wheel of the year is a modern concept. Still, as you become more attuned with nature, you may find the sabbats make more sense to you than modern holidays.

WICCA IS AN EARTH-BASED RELIGION THAT EMBRACES MAGICK.

INVESTIGATING THE SABBATS

The dates of the solstices and equinoxes vary every year, depending on astrological timing. I suggest consulting a reliable resource for the exact dates each year. *The Farmer's Almanac* or *Old Moore's Almanack* are wonderful options.

✳ YULE ✳

Northern hemisphere: 21–22 December.
Southern hemisphere: 20–21 June.

The winter solstice, also called Yule or midwinter, is the first spoke of the wheel.

According to *The Merriam Webster* dictionary, Yule originates from the Old English word *geōl*, meaning Christmas time. *Geōl* is closely related to the Norse word *jól*, a 12-day pagan festival celebrated by ancient Germanic pagans (Vikings). *Jól* was assimilated into Christmas by Christians in the early middle ages.

The winter solstice is the longest night and shortest day of the year. Though Yule is a time of darkness, it is also a time of hope and rebirth. After this day, the days grow longer, as the Sun returns. In Wiccan lore, Yule celebrates the birth and return of the Horned God, who is associated with the Sun. Does the birth of the Sun (son) in late December sound familiar? Many Christmas traditions, such as lighting a Yule log or lights in trees, originate from Yule.

Yule is a time of feasting, hibernation and gratitude. Overall energy is low, as days are at their shortest. Don't feel guilty for feeling unmotivated during the winter solstice. Before capitalism and electricity, people slept in and rested during this darker period of the year.

Make a Yule log
This is an appropriate way to celebrate Yule.

- Go into nature and find a large log. If that's not possible, a large stick can be used, or even a log purchased from a store.
- Carve or write words or sigils into the log. You can also tie petitions and wishes to the yule log with string.
- Start a fire in your fireplace or in a firepit outside. Place the log on the fire with intention. Offer cheers and thanks as you watch the flames.
- If you decide to use a real tree for your holiday decorations, you can save the trunk for the next year's Yule log.

✷ IMBOLC/IMBOLG ✷

Northern hemisphere: 1 February.
Southern hemisphere: 1 August.

The next spoke is Imbolc, sometimes called Brigid's Day. The etymology of Imbolc is uncertain. Most commonly, it is believed to originate from the old Irish *imbolg*, meaning 'in the belly', as in, a pregnant sheep. Brigid is a powerful and ancient Irish goddess. Fire, poetry, childbirth and domesticated animals are all associated with Brigid.

The halfway point between the winter solstice and the spring equinox, Imbolc signals the coming spring. The Sun begins to return and the snow starts to thaw. New plans are made, as we wake up from the hibernation of winter. In Wiccan lore, the Horned God is now in his infancy, and the Goddess has recovered from birthing him at Yule.

To celebrate, go for a walk in nature and look for signs of spring. For a simple craft, find five sticks of a similar length. Using either twine (more aesthetic) or a glue gun (way easier), form the sticks into a pentagram. Place your natural pentagram on your altar (pages 116–117) or somewhere you will see it every day.

✳ SPRING EQUINOX (OSTARA) ✳

Northern hemisphere: 20–21 March.
Southern hemisphere: 22–23 September.

On the spring equinox, called Ostara, day and night are of equal length. This equinox is the official beginning of spring, and coincides with the start of Aries season. Aries, the first sign in the zodiac, is a sign of new beginnings. Baby animals start to appear, and birds are heard chirping in the sky, finally returning from their winter migration.

Ostara is named after the Germanic goddess of spring, Ēostre, whose celebrations focus on fertility, new beginnings and rebirth. The links between Ostara and Easter are relatively new. Jacob Grimm, of Grimm's fairy tale fame, connected the goddess Ostara and the Easter holiday in his 1835 book *Deutsche Mythologie*. In Wiccan lore, the Horned God is now an adolescent. He and the Goddess share their fertility, dancing through the fields and bringing abundance.

Ostara egg dyeing
To celebrate, try dyeing eggs with a witchy twist.

You will need: An egg-dyeing kit, something to write with (markers or paint if you're crafty) and eggs.

- Hard-boil the eggs, and prepare the dye according to the package instructions.
- Decide how you want to spell your eggs, and dye them according to the colour correspondence (page 88). Dye the egg green for abundance, red for passionate love, and so on. Write or paint affirmations, symbols and petitions on your egg. For example, for a protection spell, you could dye the egg black, write 'my home is protected', and draw a pentacle. Add any stickers or additional decorations of choice. Store them in the fridge, and eat within the week.

✷ BELTANE (MAY DAY) ✷

Northern hemisphere: 30 April–1 May.
Southern hemisphere: 31 October–1 November.

The next spoke, Beltane (the anglicized pronunciation is bell-tayne, but byowl-tinuh is closer to the Irish pronunciation), is a traditional Gaelic fire festival. Occurring between the spring equinox and summer solstice, Beltane celebrates the peak of spring. Sometimes referred to as May Day, Beltane means 'bright fire' in Gaelic.

Fittingly, Beltane occurs in Taurus season – a time of growth, fertility and creation. Beltane customs revolve around flowers, greenery and raunchy themes. Phallic symbolism is common around Beltane (he-yo). Maypoles are erected and danced around. Many communities honour a young woman with the title of May Queen, representing youthful beauty and fertility. In Wiccan lore, Beltane is when the Horned God, now mature, impregnates the Goddess (it's a metaphor and not incestuous at all).

Traditionally, two bonfires were lit and livestock passed between them for cleansing and protection. If you have any pets, honour this old tradition by making them walk between two candles.

Make a flower crown

To celebrate, try making a flower crown.

You will need wire, tape and flowers.

- Go for a walk in nature, gathering wildflowers and greenery.
- To make a sturdy crown, cut a piece of floral wire in a hoop shape. Tape the ends together, and wrap the exposed wire with floral tape. If you just want your crown for the day, you can skip this step. It is harder, but not impossible, to form the flower crown without a base, but you'll need to use flowers with thicker stems.
- Using strategic knots or floral tape, if you're using a wire, fasten the flowers around in a circle. Crown yourself May Queen and dance around outside.

✷ SUMMER SOLSTICE ✷ (MIDSUMMER/LITHA)

Northern hemisphere: 20–21 June.
Southern hemisphere: 21–22 December.

The summer solstice, sometimes called Litha or midsummer, is the longest day of the year. The summer solstice celebrates the peak of the Sun's energy. In Wiccan lore, the fertility of the God and Goddess is at its peak.

With the passing of the summer solstice, days become shorter and temperatures begin to drop (at least, they did before climate change). Despite its name, midsummer is not in the middle of summer for every region. Officially, the summer solstice is the beginning of summer.

A time of abundance and increase, midsummer celebrates the Sun, fertility and the bounty of the land. Hand-fasting ceremonies are often held on midsummer. During this ancient Celtic ritual, a rope is knotted around a married couple's hands to symbolically bind them. The concept of using cords and knots for binding is frequently used in spellwork.

To celebrate midsummer, burn your ex in a bear skin (kidding). Harvest herbs to use in your magickal practice. Herbs harvested on this day are said to be at their highest power. If you work with the fae (do so at your own risk), midsummer is considered a powerful day to commune with the fairy folk.

The summer solstice is often celebrated by lighting a bonfire. If you make a fire, you can use it to do a burning releasing ritual. For this simple ritual, write something you want to release on a piece of paper (stress, anxiety or all those negative vibes) and cast it into the fire.

✳ LUGHNASADH (LAMMAS) ✳

Northern hemisphere: 1 August.
Southern hemisphere: 1 February.

Originating in Ireland, Lughnasadh (pronounced Loo na-sa, emphasis on the 'loo'), gets its name from the Gaelic deity Lugh. Lugh is a Celtic god of craftsmanship, games, mastery and more. Traditionally, Lughnasadh is held from sundown on 31 July through to sundown on 1 August.

Occurring halfway between the summer solstice and autumn equinox, Lughnasadh is the first major harvest festival. Historically, it was widely observed throughout Ireland, Scotland and the Isle of Man.

As Christianity spread through Europe, Lughnasadh evolved into Lammas, meaning 'loaf mass'. Bread was often baked, as this time aligns with the harvest of grain. The Sun's energy begins to decrease, with the promise of the larger harvests on the horizon. In Wiccan lore, the Horned God's power wanes, as the Goddess continues to swell with child (also the God – it's a metaphor, remember?).

To celebrate, bake a loaf of bread, or cook something with flour. If you're a mediocre baker like me, you can use a packaged mix. Not every ritual needs to be from scratch. Using modern conveniences doesn't make you any less of a witch.

✷ AUTUMN EQUINOX (MABON) ✷

Northern hemisphere: 22–23 September.
Southern hemisphere: 20–21 March.

The autumn equinox is the second harvest festival. Often referred to as Mabon (pronounced map-on), this sabbat marks the beginning of fall. Fittingly, it is the first day of the Libra season, when day and night are equally balanced.

In my own practice, I drop the Mabon name and simply call this sabbat the autumn equinox. The Welsh god, Mab, was not associated with this holiday until Aidan Kelly decided so in the late 1900s. Food for thought.

In Wiccan lore, the God prepares for his imminent death. The Goddess is now ripe with child (beginning her last trimester, considering he is reborn in three months at Yule).

In Greek mythology, the autumn equinox is when Persephone returns to the underworld. Her mother is Demeter, the goddess of the harvest. In her sadness, Demeter kills all crops and ushers in the beginning of winter. Try eating pomegranates on this sabbat to honour Persephone.

Make an apple candle holder
This could be an attractive Mabon decoration.

You will need: An apple, a knife, a spoon and a tealight candle.

- Using the knife, cut the bottom of the apple so it sits flat. Then, cut a circle a little larger than the candle in the top of the apple. Using the spoon, dig out the circle so the candle fits snugly.
- Be careful here – never light a candle on something that is wobbly.
- Light the candle and give thanks for the harvest and fall season. Compost or bury it afterwards, as cut fruit moulds quickly.

✷ SAMHAIN ✷

Northern hemisphere: 31 October–1 November.
Southern hemisphere: 30 April–1 May.

Samhain (pronounced SOW-in – sow as in 'plough'– not 'sam-hayne'), is the last harvest festival. Called the witch's new year, Samhain is the last spoke on the wheel, before the death and subsequent rebirth of Yule. Samhain is one of the four Gaelic fire festivals. Customarily, bonfires were lit and tended to all night.

The length of night increases as the Sun weakens. In Wiccan lore, this is when the Horned God dies, gone until the Goddess rebirths him at Yule.

To celebrate, set out a plate for relatives and friends who have passed on. Add their names to a placard so that they may live on within you. Divination is also commonly practised on Samhain. The veil between the living and dead is said to be at its thinnest. If Ouija boards are your thing, go for it (not for me, thanks).

Apple peel divination
If you're looking for love, try an apple peel divination.

You will need: An apple and a sharp knife.

- Peel an apple in one long piece and throw it over your left shoulder.
- It is said that the initials, or even the figure, of your true love will appear in the peel.

And so the wheel turns.

Common Correspondences

Correspondences help you determine what to use and when. An item's correspondence is based on a number of things: its colour, how it is used and what it is made of are all factors. It's important to note that correspondences are not set in stone. What significance a colour has for you is more important than any assigned correspondence. If you want to use a pink candle for hexing, go for it. Below is a list of basic correspondences. As you practise your craft, you may form different associations. As with everything witchy, take what resonates, and leave what doesn't. I won't be offended, I promise. Write a list of your own personal correspondences in your book of shadows.

✷ COLOURS ✷

Red	Passion, sex, action, fire.
Pink	Self-love, friendship, beauty, emotional healing.
Orange	Confidence, creativity, career, success.
Yellow	Optimism, luck, prosperity, happiness.
Green	Prosperity, abundance, fertility, nature.
Blue	Healing, communication, wisdom, evil-eye protection.
Purple	Divination, power, mastery, justice.
White	Cleansing, purity, innocence, truth.
Black	Protection, banishing, closure, transformation.
Brown	Animals, nature, grounding, earth.
Grey	Neutralizing, anonymity, secrets, reversing.

Colour correspondence exercise

In this exercise, you will define your association with each colour. Creating meaningful associations will supercharge your spellwork.

You will need: Items of different colours (such as a make-up palette or a box of coloured pencils – or you can just look up pictures of each colour online), paper and a pen.

- Take three deep breaths.
- Pick a colour at random. Focus on it. What do you think of when you see the colour? Maybe an animal, person or place comes to mind. Does the colour make you feel anything?
- Write your findings in your book of shadows.
- When that feels complete, move on to the next colour.

Do this for as many colours as you like.

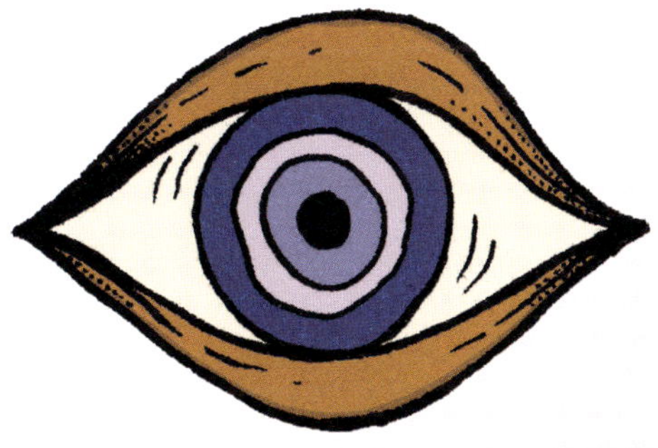

THE ELEMENTS

To recap, the four elements are earth, air, fire and water, and each one is associated with zodiac signs and the energies of the world.

EARTH

The earth element consists of the physical world around us. It is associated with material wealth, stability, money, abundance and fertility. The ground we walk on and the crystals we collect are all manifestations of the earth element. In tarot (page 92), the earth element corresponds with the suit of Pentacles.

Taurus, Virgo and **Capricorn** are associated with earth.

AIR

The element of air is associated with intellect, communication, logic, movement and thought: the oxygen we breathe, the words we speak, the decisions we make. All these are manifestations of the air element. In tarot, the air element corresponds with the suit of Swords.

Gemini, Libra and **Aquarius** are associated with air.

FIRE

The element of fire is associated with passion, action, impulse, energy and destruction. Warm bodies on a cold winter night, or the spark of a gas stove cooking your dinner: these are manifestations of the fire element. Fire is often used to banish or destroy. In tarot, the fire element corresponds with the suit of Wands.

Aries, Leo and **Sagittarius** are associated with fire.

WATER

The element of water is associated with emotions, intuition, spirituality, flow and purification. A moonlit high tide, the tears we cry, the drip of wax down a candle: all these are manifestations of the water element. In tarot, the water element corresponds with the suit of Cups.

Cancer, Scorpio and **Pisces** are associated with water.

AETHER

All energy is connected through a fifth element known as aether or spirit. The idea of aether was introduced by the ancient Greek philosopher, Aristotle. The fifth point on a pentagram represents aether.

Cardinal Directions

The points of the compass also have traditional correspondences.

- **North:** Associated with the earth element and the dark of night.
- **South:** Associated with the fire element and the day being at its peak.
- **East:** Associated with the air element; the Sun rises and the day begins in the east.
- **West:** Associated with the water element; the Sun sets and the day ends in the west. In ancient Egypt, the west was associated with death.

The Tarot

This is way beyond the scope of this book, but you'll have heard about tarot and I've mentioned it a few times, so I feel I owe you a quick definition here. Originating in Italy, early tarot decks were used as playing cards. Now, tarot is one of the most widespread forms of divination.

The tarot is a deck of cards, divided into the Major Arcana – 22 cards with specific images associated with particular energies – and the Minor Arcana, which consists of four suits of cards – Wands, Swords, Cups and Pentacles – with cards numbered ace (one) to ten as well as a Page, Knight, Queen and King in each suit. A tarot reading answers a specific question. The shuffled cards are laid out in a designated pattern, with each position relating to an aspect of the question and each card suggesting how that can be understood and acted upon.

The simplest tarot spread is a three-card, 'past, present, future' reading. Don't be afraid to learn the symbolism as you go – I've been reading tarot all my life (thanks, Dad!) and still look things up occasionally.

Hands & Feet

How we interact with the world is expressed through our hands. Generally in witchcraft, the left hand is used for receiving and the right hand is for giving. Switch this if you are left-hand dominant.

Our feet are where energy exits the body. Growing up, my Thai mom always yelled at me when I pointed the soles of my feet towards an elder. In Thai custom, your feet are the dirtiest part of the body. It is considered highly disrespectful to point your feet at anyone. This is why Thai people often sit on their knees with their feet tucked behind them, especially in temples.

Clockwise & Counterclockwise

If you are particularly handy, you will have heard the phrase, 'righty tighty, lefty loosey'. Twisting to the right will tighten a screw, and twisting to the left will loosen it. The same concept applies in witchcraft. Clockwise is for bringing in or invoking. Counterclockwise is for removing or banishing. You know: wax on, wax off.

When cleansing an object or surface, wipe in a counterclockwise direction first. Focus on removing anything you don't wish to remain. This applies not just in rituals but also in daily life. Then clean in a clockwise direction, while focusing on the intention you wish to bring in.

Cleansing & Protection

Spiritual Cleansing

Protection and cleansing go hand in hand. Protecting without cleansing seals in both wanted and unwanted energies. Cleansing without protecting allows negative energies to build back up. Just as doctors sanitize a room before surgery, it is necessary to cleanse oneself and one's space before performing magick. You wouldn't go a week without a shower (hopefully). Keep up with spiritual hygiene practices in a similar vein.

Witches know that just because something appears clean, doesn't mean it's energetically sound. Follow mundane cleaning with spiritual cleansing. An item can be clear of grime, but still hold onto unpleasant energies.

✷ SMOKE CLEANSING ✷

Smoke cleansing cleanses with smoke. Pretty self-explanatory. Waft the smoke into every nook and cranny. When smoke cleansing a room, don't forget to open the cabinets and drawers.

INCENSE

A herbal paste that is formed around either a stick or a cone, burn incense to cleanse a space, yourself, or as an offering to your ancestors. In my opinion, this is the easiest method of smoke cleansing.

SMOKE BUNDLES

Bundles of dried herbs can be tied together with twine and burned for smoke cleansing. These are normally 'smokier' than a regular incense stick, and it is harder to keep them lit. If you have trouble re-lighting a smoke bundle, try breaking off all the burned bits. Or say, 'screw it' and chuck the whole thing into the fire.

HERBS FOR SMOKE CLEANSING

- **Juniper:** Smoke cleansing with juniper is a traditional Scottish method of purification, called saining.
- **Rosemary:** Used for protection, cleansing and healing. As a bonus, rosemary smoke repels mosquitos. Literal protection in action!
- **Sage:** Regular garden sage, not white sage (page 27).
- **Mugwort:** Used to enhance dreams, meditation and divination.

INSTANT WITCH TIP – Smoke cleansing

Always open a window (at least one; two is better) when smoke cleansing to allow energy to escape. Keep your pets away from any fumes as it is bad for their tiny lungs.

✷ SOUND CLEANSING ✷

Sound cleansing works using vibration to move stagnant energy. Really get in there – move your tool a full 360 degrees around any item you wish to sound cleanse. Don't forget to do the back!

- **Bells:** Every time a bell rings, an angel gets its wings. Even in pop culture, bells have a positive connotation. The crisp, clear ding of a bell creates a pleasing melody, perfect for moving energy around a space.
- **Singing bowls**: A metal bowl, often used in meditation, that produces a pleasant tone when struck.

CLOSET WITCH TIP – Play some music

Put on your favourite music for sneaky sound cleansing.

EVERY TIME A BELL RINGS, AN ANGEL GETS ITS WINGS.

✷ CLEANSING CRYSTALS ✷

When you first acquire a crystal, cleanse it thoroughly. The simplest way to clean a crystal is passing it under running water – aka your tap or faucet. Look up a crystal's water solubility before cleaning it with water – crystals that end in 'ite' (selenite, calcite, etc) generally should not get wet. Alternatively, you can submerge the crystal in salt, or bury it in the ground for a few days. White or clear crystals typically have cleansing properties.

- **Selenite:** A form of gypsum (like chalk), selenite is known for its purifying, protective and healing properties. Place magickal items on a selenite plate to cleanse and charge them. Hit someone with a selenite wand to get them to leave (kidding).
- **Clear quartz:** A versatile crystal, clear quartz promotes clarity, amplifies and can even draw out negative energies. Place clear quartz on your desk to improve focus, or next to your favourite crystal to multiply its effect.

No tools, no problem
If you're caught without any tools, use your hands to shift the energy of a space. Clap in each corner of a room or space, going in a counterclockwise direction.

✷ SPIRITUAL MIASMA ✷

In Greek polytheism, there exists the concept of spiritual miasma. Miasma roughly translates as pollution. We accumulate spiritual miasma going about our lives. This can be through our environment, or by behaving in ways that do not align with our highest good. Methods of escapism, like drugs and alcohol, leave behind miasma.

Spiritual cleansing techniques aim to clear this miasma. Mundane cleansing methods, such as taking a shower or ritual bath, should be employed in tandem. You can't ring a bell to replace a shower, for example.

✷ RITUAL BATH ✷

Ritual baths are one of the oldest forms of magickal cleansing. Soaking in water relaxes the nervous system and resets your emotional state. A ritual bath can even be strong enough to remove a hex or jinx (pages 137–141). To do that, take a bath for an odd number of days in a row, at least three, ideally in the morning.

Take ritual baths as often as you can. Even if it's just for ten minutes. Baths calm the parasympathetic nervous system. I have sensitive skin and will sometimes do one with only plain salt, Epsom salt and a few drops of oil.

Start by cleansing your bathroom as usual. Cleanse spiritually, using tools such as smoke bundles, incense, bells or singing bowls. Cleanse yourself normally – you should be clean before entering a ritual bath. Select your chosen herbs and salt (see below) and place in a sachet. Draw the ritual bath. Do not towel yourself off after a ritual bath; let the water dry on your skin. Stand in front of a fan if you need to dry quickly.

Here are some ideas for what to add to your bath.

- **Protection:** Salt, rosemary, lavender.
- **Cleansing:** Salt, black salt, lemon.
- **Love:** Rose petals, jasmine, pink salt.

RITUAL SHOWER

Turn your normal shower into one that is spiritually cleansing by setting the intention of the water purifying you, and any negative energy being washed away. I like to visualize this as black sludge rinsing down the drain. When you step out of the shower, envision a white light purifying your body. Walk out of the shower as you walk into the best version of yourself.

Protection

Protection starts at the most essential needs, like having a safe place to sleep and knowing where your next meal is coming from. Eating your vegetables can offer more protection than a black candle. If you're exhausted, casting a spell will weaken you more, leaving you vulnerable to negative energies. Think of practical remedies, then reinforce them with witchy protection.

Very rarely will you be under psychic attack by a spiritual practitioner. Most of the time, negative energy is sent inadvertently. The person you cut off in traffic, a friend who doesn't mean well or a nosy neighbour can all send negative energy your way. If you're not prone to headaches, a sharp pang of pain in the centre of your forehead is an obvious sign of psychic attack.

Energetic protection keeps your energy yours, shielded from negative influences. This section focuses on protecting your person. More information on protecting your space can be found in the chapter on House Witchcraft (pages 106–121).

Imagine you're in a café. Someone enters in a hurry, and slams their backpack on the table next to you. They mutter angrily to themselves. Without protection, you might pick up some of their energy. You may find yourself getting annoyed or distracted from your own work.

Using spiritual protection and grounding techniques, you protect your inner balance.

Herbs for protection
Rosemary, lavender, St John's wort, garlic (technically a vegetable).

Smoke cleanse with these herbs, make sachets (did you know it's pronounced 'sa-shay' and not 'sat-chet'? I certainly didn't until embarrassingly recently) and place them throughout your home, or just straight up eat garlic. Garlic has antimicrobial properties and keeps away more than just vampires.

✷ ENERGY VAMPIRES ✷

If you always leave a conversation with someone feeling drained, you may be dealing with an energy vampire.

Energy vampires take and do not give. They are people who ask for favour after favour and offer nothing in return. Or they vent to you about the same ex, but their eyes turn glassy when you talk about your problems.

When dealing with an energy vampire, the best technique is known as 'grey rocking'. Invoke the spirit of a grey rock: unmoving, unnoticeable, uncaring. Divulge few details about your life, and reply using short, noncommittal phrases. If you use this technique, an energy vampire will eventually give up and move onto their next target.

✷ EVIL EYE ✷

Many cultures believe in a concept known as the evil eye, *mallochio* or *mal de ojo*, which is the idea that jealousy can inadvertently cause a curse. Keep your wins close to your chest. When in doubt, it's best to keep quiet. If you are about to share something and hear a ringing in your ear, change the subject. Ringing in your ears is often a warning, unless you suffer from tinnitus. Strong ringing could mean someone is sending a large amount of negative energy your way. Unexplained sluggishness, bad luck and headaches can also be signs of the evil eye. Please exhaust mundane explanations first – not everything has a spiritual cause. Sometimes you just have a bad day.

You've probably seen the blue, white and black eye emoji. Fun fact – that symbol is not an 'evil eye', it is called a nazar. Nazar amulets are commonly used to repel the evil eye. In some cultures, a nazar talisman is most powerful when gifted. In my eyes, buying one with your man's card counts as gifted. Wear it as jewellery, hang it in your home, or place it wherever you need protection. I have one attached to my car keys so it's always with me. When a nazar breaks, that means it caught negative energy sent your way. Throw it away and get a new one. Don't try to fix or reuse it.

Egg cleanses are common in many folk practices. A note on terminology: '*limpia con/de huevo*' is a closed practice, originating in indigenous Latin America. Egg cleanses are to *limpias* as smoke cleansing is to smudging (page 27). If you're not a *brujx* (a practitioner of Latin-American folk magick), this is called an egg cleanse.

How to do an egg cleanse

If you think someone has given you the evil eye, try doing an egg cleanse.

You will need: An egg, salt and a glass of water. Use a designated glass for egg cleanses; don't drink out of it afterwards.

- Fill the glass with water, add a teaspoonful of salt, and allow it to come to room temperature. Clean the egg while focusing on your intention.
- Hold the egg and meditate or pray over it for a few minutes.
- Gently rub the egg all over your body, starting at the head and moving down. While rubbing, force any negative energy out of your body and into the egg.
- Crack the egg into the glass of water and wait ten minutes for it to settle. Never look down at the egg from above; always read it from the side. The shape the egg takes can be indicative of negative energies such as the evil eye or gossip.

Reading an egg cleanse

- **Bubbles:** Success – you have cleansed the evil eye.
- **Strings:** Karmic cords (invisible energy ties we have to other people).
- **Cloudiness:** Sickness, fogginess or a physical issue.

- **Spikes:** Gossip.
- **An eye:** A surefire sign of the evil eye. And if it's bloody or weird coloured, oh boy! Do a full evil eye removal.
- **Faces or figures:** They may be sending you negative energy.
- **Blood:** Someone may have successfully cast the evil eye on you.

Dispose of the egg cleanse by flushing it down the toilet. You can optionally add vinegar and hot peppers to return the evil to its sender. I personally don't, because the people who most often give you the evil eye are loved ones who don't do it intentionally.

✷ PROTECTION BRAID ✷

Also called prayer braids, protection braids are a simple form of energetic protection. You may have mindlessly done one of these before knowing their spiritual purposes. They are braids created with the intention of protecting yourself from other people's energy, and are especially useful before large events or going out in public. Protection braids are easily customizable depending on the intention set or oil used.

Separate a small section of hair at the nape of your neck. Divide into three equal sections. Plait normally, while focusing on the intention of protection. You can even speak protective affirmations into the braid, such as:

- I am divinely protected.
- I transmute any negative energy for my greatest good.
- No one's energy can affect mine.

When you're finished, anoint the braid with oil. Rosemary, which already has the correspondence of protection, is a wonderful option. When you are out and about, any negative energy will be trapped in the braid. When you come home, release the braid. Imagine any negative energy evaporating from the braid as black smoke. If the protection braid has become sticky, matted or dirty, that means it absorbed an especially large amount of bad energy. In that case, immediately wash your hair.

HOUSE WITCHCRAFT

LIVING IN A WITCH'S HOUSE

A WITCH'S HOME IS said to be alive – a collection of spirits, energies and magickal objects. Not every witch's house is Baba Yaga's hut, nestled in the deep forest on chicken legs (google it if this doesn't ring any bells). Mine basically is, but that's because I've buried so many chickens on the property (if you raise chickens, you know how tragically fragile they are).

Your home is where you rest and recharge. If you've ever lived in a toxic environment, you know how draining that can be.

When I say home, I don't mean a freestanding building with four walls. Living in an apartment, a shared space, your car or nowhere at all does not make you any less of a witch. Home is where the heart is, as they say.

✷ HOUSE SPIRIT ✷

Give your home a name. Keep it secret (keep it safe), and don't tell it to anyone, especially another spiritual practitioner. Names have power – you wouldn't want someone hexing your house!

Treat your home as if it is a member of the family. Say goodbye when you leave, hello when you return, and tuck it in at night. Talk to it like it has feelings.

Designate a small altar space to your house spirit and leave it regular offerings. This might be cream, a small portion of anything you cook, honey, wine, cookies, fruit or vegetables.

✷ SPIRIT OF THE LAND ✷

Every area has a spirit – or a 'vibe', if spirit is too woo for you. If you're reading this, hopefully it's not. The spirit of a place is a combination of all the people who have lived there and the events that have occurred there.

Emotional events leave echoes. A hole in drywall from a fist. A shard of glass from a broken bottle. Through both physical and spiritual cleansings, we can work to clear these echoes and replace them with our own, positive vibrations.

Working with the spirit of the land is your first line of defence. If you notice something off, like unexplained dead animals, or piles of cigarette butts, redo your protections. Check in with the spirit of your land at least quarterly (another thing to time with the solstices and equinoxes). A simple way to connect with this spirit is to sit outside.

✷ MOVING ✷

Finding the perfect space can be quite the endeavour. When in the market, one of the homes I viewed had a pile of dead flies in the basement. Needless to say, I did not put in an offer. If your gut is telling you about a home – listen. Horror movie rules. This applies to anything, really. If the vibes are off, you'll never see me again.

Schedule a few days of overlap so you can do purification rituals before actually moving. Introduce yourself to your new home. Tell anything that is not for your highest good to GTFO. Take a few minutes to meditate, and leave an offering for the house spirit. Be intuitive with your offering; there are some ideas on the previous page.

Cleanse while the space is empty, before you start moving in. Get professional cleaners if you can, or spend a few days deep cleaning. Make sure to get into every crevice. Open cabinets and drawers, and even get down drains. The night before you move in, place bowls of salt water in the middle of each room. This will absorb negative energy.

Avoid bringing an old broom to a new place. Brooms carry energy. Leave your old broom for the next person. If you're really attached to it, turn your old broom into an outside-only broom. And if you must continue using the same broom, cleanse and repair it thoroughly.

Scribing exercise
An exercise to decide if a home is the right one for you.

You will need: Paper and a pen.

- Write the street address of the home you are considering on a piece of paper. Write it as many times as it takes to fill the paper.
- As you write, imagine your life in the space: waking up there, cooking, chilling out. Let your mind wander. By the time the paper is full, you should have a good idea of whether or not the home is for you.

✷ APARTMENTS & SHARED SPACES ✷

In a shared home, use your bedroom door as your front door for rituals. Take extra precautions to protect shared walls. You can draw protective symbols, like pentacles, on them with spiritual liquid moonwater (pages 64–65), Florida water (page 115) or even spit.

Avoid leaving blood in shared bathrooms., especially if you know the owner of said trash can is a spiritualist, or if any spiritualists have access to it.

Do a protection braid (page 105) or some form of veiling before entering the lift or common areas, especially if you are a woman alone. Veiling is the practice of covering the crown. For basic veiling, use a scarf, hoodie or baseball cap.

CLOSET WITCH TIP – Simmer pots

Simmer pots are a subtle way to switch up the energy of common areas, especially after an argument. To make a simple simmer pot, add fruit peels, cinnamon, salt and water to a small pot and simmer on your stove.

✷ DOORS ✷

Doors are portals. Doorways are liminal spaces. You've likely walked across a threshold and completely forgotten what you were doing. Your door is your last line of defence. Anything that can penetrate your door is now in your space.

Hang a horseshoe above your front door for luck. Different cultures position it both ways. You can hang it upright as a 'u' to hold luck in, or position the horseshoe downwards to spill luck on whoever enters. Hang bells from your door handles for sound cleansing when anyone comes and goes.

PURPLE DOORS

In modern times, witches and pagans paint their doors purple to indicate that they practise magick. This doesn't have any historical significance, but who doesn't love purple?

CLOSET WITCH TIP – Doors indoors

If you're in the broom closet, or somewhere it's not safe to openly announce your witchiness, paint an interior door purple, both in solidarity with others who practise the craft, and to add a mystical touch to your space.

✷ MONEY CORNER ✷

The money corner is borrowed from feng shui and is the optimal position for anything to do with finances, where you should place a small altar or money bowl. A money bowl is simple and encourages your money to work for you. To find your money corner, start at your front door. Walk all the way to the back of the space, and all the way to the left. If this corner doesn't work, by your front entrance is also a good place to put it. Really, anywhere that is pet safe, and ideally out of eyeshot from outside, for security.

✷ MIRRORS ✷

Have you ever walked by a mirror, especially at night, and felt a weird vibe? If you ever walk past a mirror and something feels off about the reflection, it's time to lock it. Many cultures believe mirrors are portals, or that spirits can become trapped in them. That's why mirrors are often covered when someone dies. To prevent this, you can lock your mirrors, which is essentially cleansing and protecting them spiritually. When used properly, mirrors are a powerful spiritual tool – and nothing to be afraid of.

How to lock a mirror

Locking a mirror prevents negative spiritual energy affecting your home.

You will need: Cleaning materials and spiritual cleansing items.

- To lock a mirror, clean the mirror as usual. I like to do everything in threes, but feel free to pick a number that resonates. Clean counterclockwise your chosen number of times, using your normal cleaning product.
- Next, spiritually cleanse the mirror. You can use smoke, such as incense or a smoke bundle. If you can't smoke cleanse, you can use bells, singing bowls or music. Go counterclockwise three times, while focusing on banishing anything negative. Then go clockwise three times while focusing on the intention you want to bring in.
- Finally, lock the mirror. Use a spiritual liquid, such as moonwater (pages 64–65), to draw protective symbols on the mirror. I normally do a pentacle on the sides and centre (crosses, stars or an 'x' are some other ideas). If you like, use a physical key and mime the mirror locking. Redo this whenever it feels right, at least quarterly.

There is debate around whether this only applies to 'silver-backed' mirrors, or if it includes black mirrors, such as televisions. If in doubt, it doesn't hurt to lock anything reflective.

MIRROR PLACEMENT

Placement of mirrors is just as important as locking them. Mirrors reflect and amplify whatever they are facing. Mirrors opposite the front door can push energy out of the home. Instead, position a mirror at a right angle to your front door. Avoid reflecting clutter. Point mirrors towards aesthetic areas, like sources of natural light or greenery.

✷ CLUTTER ✷

A cluttered space reflects a cluttered mind. As above, so below. Nothing invites new in more than an empty shelf or cabinet. This is why keeping your home clean, both in mundane and spiritual terms, is so important.

Physically clean before moving onto spiritual cleansing methods. Ringing a bell won't do anything if you're covered in mud. The time spent smoke cleansing a pile of clutter would be better used resolving it.

✷ FLOOR WASHES ✷

The floor is arguably the most important part of the home to keep clean. Growing up in an Asian household, leaving shoes on inside was considered a cardinal sin. And nothing beats getting down on your hands and knees and scrubbing with intention.

- Wash from the back to the front to repel or push out.
- Wash from the front to the back to attract or bring in.
- Start at the top floor to repel.
- Start at the bottom floor to attract.
- Pour dirty water out of the front door and to the east.

For extra spiritual cleansing, add a few drops of Florida water to the mopping solution.

FLORIDA WATER ✷ SPIRITUAL COLOGNE ✷

No, Florida water is not water from Florida. Florida water is an alcohol-based spiritual cologne, used in many hoodoo and folk magick practices. The most commonly used Florida water was first released as a perfume by Murray and Lanman in 1808. It has a light floral scent and powerful cleansing properties. It is often used when a spiritual liquid is needed. Be careful when using Florida water on wooden surfaces, as it may strip them (RIP my antique side table). You can buy Florida water at your local metaphysical store, online or at some big-box retailers in the perfume section. They even sell it at Walmart, for my American witches (booo corporations, but yay, accessible Florida water).

SOS – GET RID OF NEGATIVE ENERGY

If someone with a bad vibe has been in your space, you need to get rid of the negative energy. Sprinkle salt in the corners and leave it for a few hours before you sweep it up. You can also light a white candle when they leave.

✷ WINDOWS ✷

Windows both allow light in and allow people to see in. When cleaning your windows, shine with the intention of mental clarity. As you remove smudges, you remove mental fog.

NOSY NEIGHBOURS

Weave two needles in the shape of a St Andrew's cross into your curtains. Point the sharp ends towards the direction of peeping eyes. Be careful placing needles if you have kids or pets. I never said a witch's home is particularly childproof – mine certainly isn't.

✷ UNWANTED GUESTS ✷

Weave or tape two needles in the shape of a St Andrew's cross underneath your doormat to deter unwanted guests. Point the sharp ends away from the home.

How to create a simple home shield

Make sure to clean and cleanse your home thoroughly.

- Envision a sphere of white light enveloping your home like a bubble.
- Extend this light to the edge of your space, enclosing everything within.
- Boom! That's it; everything doesn't have to be complicated. The shield works both ways – trapping negative energy outside but containing positive energy within the home.

✷ ALTAR ✷

Spiritualists of all varieties can benefit from a designated altar space. An altar is a sacred place, where you can perform rituals, store magickal tools or connect with spirits.

All you need for an altar is a flat surface – somewhere out of reach of grubby hands or curious familiars. The top of a dresser, a bookshelf or a windowsill make fantastic altars.

Once you designate a space as your altar, only place magickal items there. No using it to place your drinks (unless you want to leave one as an offering). If you visit someone's home, please never place items on their altar or other religious space. Common sense, folks.

Creating an altar

An altar can be the focus of your spells and rituals.

- Pick a spot for your altar. Cleanse the area both mundanely and spiritually.

- Gather your materials. A basic altar incorporates all four elements: earth, air, fire and water. For example, a crystal for the earth element, feather for air, candle for fire and a cup of water for water.
- Put down an altar cloth, to cover any finishes and protect the surface from candle wax.
- Arrange your materials as you see fit. Typically, items are placed according to their associated cardinal direction, but that's certainly not required (east = air, south = fire, west = water, north = earth).
- If you wish to devote your altar to a deity, place a representation of them, such as a statue, on the altar, as well as a place for offerings.

CLOSET WITCH TIP – Mini altar

You can make a discreet mini altar in a mint tin or old glasses case.

✷ BEDROOM ✷

This area is associated with love and romance. Avoid sleeping with a mirror facing or reflecting the bed. This may cause restlessness, and you are especially vulnerable while you sleep. If this cannot be helped, cover the mirror at night.

Do not sleep with an empty chair facing your bed. It is said the dead will watch you sleep (unless that's your thing). It's also a great excuse to pile that chair with unfolded laundry.

✷ BATHROOM ✷

The bathroom is where the water element enters and exits your house, and it is associated with prosperity. If you have a bout of ill luck regarding your finances, try giving your bathroom a makeover using these tips. Add wooden touches to your bathroom to balance the Water element. Yes, a wooden squatty potty counts.

TOILET

Toilets can drain energy. Always keep the toilet lid closed. Leaving it open allows positive energy to drain from your home (quite apart from being hygienic). Also, please always close the lid before you flush. Apparently that's not common knowledge.

BATHROOM PLANTS

Add greenery, as plants purify energy (I call this greenergy). Some plants to keep in your bathroom are: ivy, snake plants, aloe, mint and spider plants. If you do not have natural light in your bathroom, you can get UV grow lights; I have purple ones. Alternatively, move plants into the room while you shower for a tropical jungle ritual shower moment.

BATHROOM ART

It is said putting pictures of people in the bathroom will bring them bad health. Think about it. Things in the bathroom are prone to mould, not to mention particles of faecal matter. Getting these on pictures of friends is not a good look. If you want to hang a picture of an enemy in the bathroom, I won't stop you.

Hang art instead. Ideally, support a local artist. Most of my art is from arts festivals.

✷ RAILROAD SPIKES ✷

Railroad spikes, made of steel, are utilized for protection in many folk-magick practices. Iron and other metals are often employed to keep away evil spirits. Actually, they were said to keep away 'witches', but nowadays, we know witches aren't all evil.

If you're lucky, you might come across a railroad spike on a hike. Alternatively, buy one at your local metaphysical store. They have the tendency to appear when you are looking for them, so keep an eye out.

Place railroad spikes at the northern, southern, eastern and western points of your property for protection.

✷ HEARTH ✷

The hearth is associated with sacred fire and vitality, and is an important energetic heart of the home. Keep the hearth free of trash and dust. If your space doesn't have a hearth, you can make a symbolic one with a candle or even play a video of a fireplace on YouTube.

My primary altar is on my mantlepiece. Every month or so, I decorate it with representations of the seasons: trinkets, candles and fruits.

✷ HOME PROTECTION TIPS ✷

- Avoid any decor that says 'welcome' or 'come on in'. Be intentional with what you invite into your home – no blanket invitations. Vampire rules, people.
- Place selenite wands above entrances to purify entering energies.
- Mix a pinch of black salt into paint. Paint protective words and sigils directly into your door.
- Place protective crystals – like black tourmaline, obsidian or black onyx – in the corners of each room.
- Mix cinnamon, black salt and eggshell powder (page 145) and sprinkle across your front and back thresholds.
- Keep both a black and a white candle near your front door for protection and purification, respectively. If you have a large gathering in your space, light both candles afterwards.
- Smoke cleanse the perimeter of your home quarterly on the solstices and equinoxes. Use this time to check for trash, signs of pests and other vulnerabilities.
- Take advice from *Practical Magic* (google it if you haven't seen the film): 'Keep rosemary by your garden gate' or front entrance. Rosemary wards off pests and has protective properties.

✷ FAMILIARS ✷

Witches, I've found, are varying degrees of animal people. I've yet to meet a witch who didn't love animals, even if they didn't have their own. If you're not an animal person, then no harm, no fowl – I simply can't relate. Furry, feathered, scaly – all friends and fine companions.

Witches are said to have companions that aid them, called familiars. Familiars are helpful spirits that often manifest physically in the form of an animal. Common familiars include cats, dogs, birds, rats and snakes.

If you ask a witch about their familiar, they'll likely point you to their cat or dog. Familiars lead short lives but can leave a profound impact. Animals are closer to nature than us. Cats especially are sensitive to spirits, and can sense energies before we do. If your familiar vibe-checks someone, listen to them.

The key difference between a familiar and a pet is energy exchange. My ride-or-die Australian Shepherd, who sounds the alarm to threats (and the mailman) is definitely a familiar. The chickens, who tolerate me merely because I feed them, bless them, are not familiars. Familiars tend to come into your life around the full moon.

To attract a familiar, light a brown candle under the full moon. If you do a spell like this, you can't really choose the species of your familiar. Be prepared to find a random wounded animal, or have a pet come to you in another unpredictable way. If you want to pick a specific familiar, take inspired action, like going to an adoption event, rather than relying on spellwork.

IF YOUR FAMILIAR
VIBE-CHECKS SOMEONE,
LISTEN TO THEM.

SPELLCRAFTING

What Are Spells?

Now we get to the real 'meat' of witchcraft. In this section, we will go over the who, what, when, where and why of spellwork. Spellwork is an art form – it's called a craft for a reason. Connect with your inner creative when designing spells.

There are limits to magick. For magick to work, it needs to be something that is physically possible. You cannot successfully cast a spell to make a fish grow wings. Spells won't achieve your goals for you. They may clear blockages and open roads along the way, but to reach your goals, you need to combine inspired action and rest with your spells.

A ritual action done with intent to achieve a result is a spell. Witches use spells to create change in the physical world, by directing energy. This is done using a variety of tools and words, or none at all. Here are the answers to some basic questions.

WHO CAN CAST A SPELL?

Anyone! Spellcasting is not specific to any gender, culture or type of witch.

WHAT IF I MESS SOMETHING UP?

If your intentions are pure, spells are very hard to mess up. That's the beauty of spellcrafting. You don't know what you don't know. A spell might not turn out exactly how you meant it, but that's the universe redirecting you. And if you miss something major, the universe will let you know. Once, I cast for abundance and received a cheque (remember them?!) in the mail for ten cents. Now, I know that specificity is key. If you don't have an exact amount in mind, add 'or something better', or a '+' sign.

WHEN TO CAST?

Consider how astrology relates to the theme of your spell. What phase is the Moon in? Are there any retrogrades? If there is a retrograde in the ruling planet of the spell (such as Venus for love spells), wait if possible.

Some spells require urgency and quick action – don't let waiting for the proper moon phase hold you back.

TYPES OF SPELL

Below are some types of spell. Feel free to experiment with different varieties, and pick your favourites. For simplicity's sake, we will focus on candle magick.

- Candle spells.
- Spell jars.
- Poppets.
- Sachets.
- Oils.
- Twine.
- Knot magick.
- Sigils.

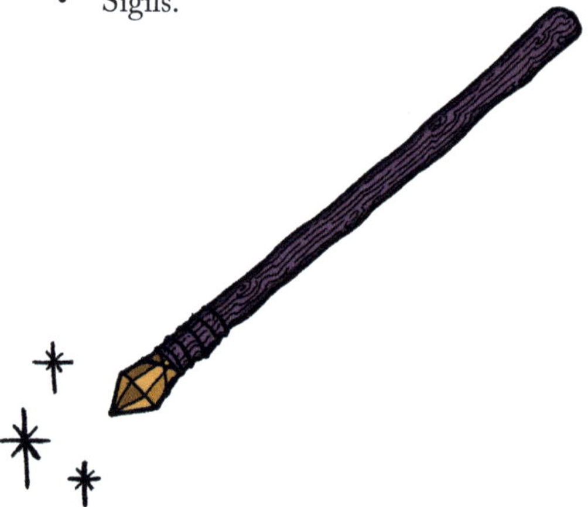

HOW TO CRAFT A SPELL

✷ DEFINE YOUR WHY ✷

Arguably the most important part of spellcraft – and the first step in creating a spell – is to define what result you are trying to achieve. The entire purpose of a spell is to influence the world to achieve a result. If there is no 'why' for your spell, you might as well do nothing. If you're looking to cast a spell simply to cast a spell, try using divination to pick an intent.

✷ CRAFT YOUR SPELL ✷

Journal for ten minutes or so. Be specific about what you want to achieve with the spell. Review your writing, and use a highlighter to mark key words and phrases.

Craft these keywords into an incantation. This is typically in AABB or ABAB rhyming format, but doesn't need to be. A few sentences work just fine. Always phrase spells in the present tense, and in a positive manner, for example: 'I am happy' instead of 'I will not be sad'. Any incantation you customize yourself will be more powerful that one you blindly follow from a spellbook.

Look up any correspondences you need to, and write down the steps you want to perform. If you're using a spell crafted by someone else, or you want to cast on the fly, you can skip this step.

✷ PREPARE YOUR INGREDIENTS ✷

Mise en place is a French cooking term meaning 'putting in place'. Gather your ingredients, pre-chop your herbs and place them in position so that when your spellwork is ready to go, you're not digging through old coat pockets for a lighter.

Sure, you can frantically grab herbs from your witch shelf in a rage (been there). But it makes for a more magickal and grounding experience to have everything intentionally set out before then. Plus, you can use all the cute little trinket dishes you've doubtlessly acquired. If you don't have any, charity shops and thrift stores are great places to check.

Infuse your energy into every component of the spell. The simplest way is to hold the items in your hands, while pushing your intention into them. If you have trouble with this, drill the energy ball exercise on pages 20–21. If praying is your thing, feel free to pray over your ingredients.

✷ RAISE ENERGY ✷

Not all the energy for your spell comes from the ingredients. An important, often overlooked, part of spellcrafting is raising energy. This is the energy you will then direct during the spell. Some ways to raise energy include dancing (twerking counts), drumming, meditating and chanting.

✷ GROUND YOURSELF ✷

After raising energy, take a few moments to ground yourself. My favourite way to ground is through a practice called earthing. Stand outside on the grass barefoot, and picture roots growing from the bottom of your feet. Breathe in, and breathe energy in from the earth and up your spine. Exhale, and release any unwanted energy back into the earth.

Cast a Circle

Casting a circle separates your magickal space from the mundane world. You don't need to do a full salt circle invoking the elements every time you cast. But doing a ritual *something* to cast a circle tells your brain that it's magick time. I always at least clean the space while envisioning a white light.

If you remember (I sometimes don't), light a black pillar candle for extra protection, especially if the spell you're casting requires lots of energy.

Witches all have their own ways of casting a circle. Remember, move clockwise for invoking, counterclockwise for banishing. Before casting a circle, find a safe space and tidy it up.

Below are a few ideas to get you started. Feel free to adapt them to your own practice.

- Sprinkle salt around the perimeter of your circle.
- Stand in what will be the centre of your circle. Extend your arm fully. Point your finger or hold your athame, and slowly rotate. Visualize a white light emanating from your chosen tool. When you return to your starting point, the circle is cast.
- Cleanse with salt water in a circular motion while envisioning a white sphere. I do this one whenever I'm working indoors on my kitchen island.

Perform the Spell

NVOKE ANY GODS or spirits you would like to call upon. I normally call upon the power of the Earth, and not a specific deity. Say the incantation, light the candle – do the dang thing. The more focused effort you put into this portion, the more potent the spell will be.

✷ CLOSING THE SPELL ✷

To close the circle when the spell is complete, start by thanking any spirits you've invoked, and respectfully asking them to depart. Then, do the reverse of whatever you did to cast the circle. For example, if you cast your circle in a clockwise motion, close it by going counterclockwise.

If you feel any excess energy remains, ground yourself again at this point.

Say, 'For the good of all and with harm to none' as a 'catch-all' to close any loopholes (only if your spell isn't meant to cause harm, of course).

Close your spell with one of the phrases below or write your own. Tell the universe, with decisiveness, that your spell is now in effect. No buts about it.

- So mote it be.
- It is so.
- So it is.
- Amen.

Write a few notes about how the spell went, then forget about it. Trust that the universe has your back.

INSTANT WITCH TIP – Fire safety

If you practise fire magick, you need to practise fire safety. Do not leave a burning candle unattended. Never light a candle close to a TV or other electronics – heat from the flame can ruin the screen – or on top of anything precious – the base of a candle can also be hot. When casting outside, survey the area for any dried foliage. If you have a cat or other mischievous familiar, keep an extra close eye on any open flames. Always light candles on a fire-safe tray, and brush off dry herbs around the wick. Keep naked flames well away from any loose fabric or curtains. Know where your nearest fire extinguisher is – you never know when you might need it.

TELL THE UNIVERSE, WITH DECISIVENESS, THAT YOUR SPELL IS NOW IN EFFECT. NO BUTS ABOUT IT.

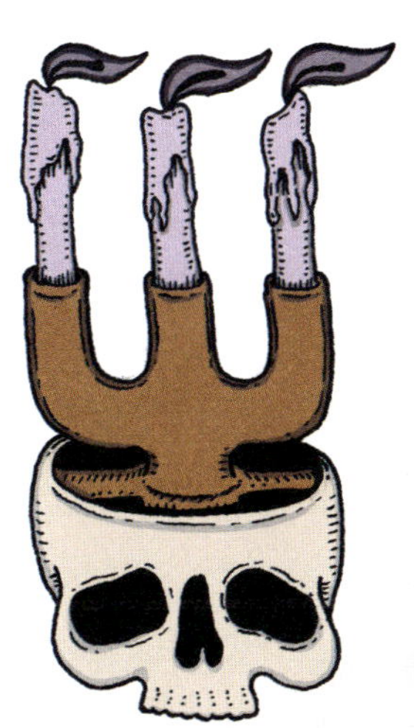

CANDLE MAGICK

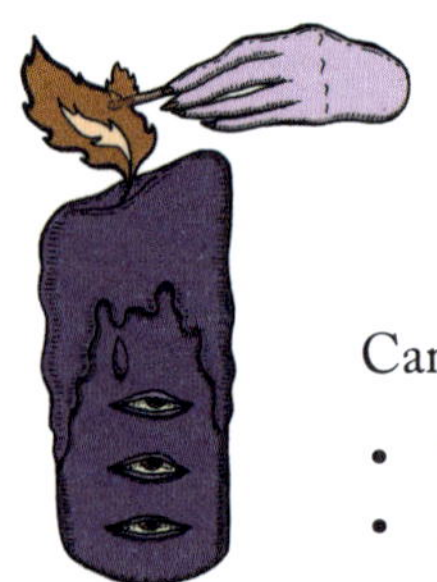

Candles represent all four elements:

- **Water** = melting wax
- **Air** = smoke
- **Earth** = wax
- **Fire** = flame

They are the simplest way to focus energy in a spell. When choosing a candle, pick one that suits the intended length of the spell. Tea lights or chime candles work well for shorter spells. Pillar candles work best for multi-day spells.

CLOSET WITCH TIP – Candles

You can use any type of candle for spells. Yes, even one from the supermarket that you quietly slipped into your trolley. To use a mundane candle, remove any stickers – especially ones that say 'warning' or 'caution' (unless that aligns with the intention of your spell).

✷ HOW TO CRAFT A CANDLE SPELL ✷

First, decide on the intention of your spell. Pick a colour of candle that corresponds with what you are trying to achieve. Use a sharp tool to carve words, names or sigils into your candle.

Anoint your candle by rubbing oil on it with intention. Rub from the bottom of the candle up to push something away. Rub from the top down to attract. Add any other spell components – herbs, salts, flowers. It is easier to get them to stick if you grind them into a powder using a mortar and pestle. Rub your additions onto the oiled candle while focusing on your intention.

To secure a candle upright, heat the bottom for a few seconds before sticking it into position. If your spell involves spoken words, say them three times before lighting the candle. Concentrate on your intention for as long as you can once the candle is lit.

Allow the candle to burn down. You don't have to do it all at once; multi-day spells can be powerful. The first time you light a candle, burn the entire top layer of wax. This prevents tunnelling – every candle aficionado's nightmare – which is when the wax forms a 'tunnel' around the wick, and doesn't melt fully.

INSTANT WITCH TIP – To snuff or not to snuff?

Some consider it disrespectful to blow out a candle. Blowing out a candle is overpowering the element of Fire with Air. Ideally, snuff out a candle with wet fingers or a candle snuffer. If you do decide to blow out a candle, take care to not blow wax everywhere.

✷ WHAT TO DO WITH OLD SPELLS ✷

- Burn in a fire-safe vessel, such as a cauldron.
- Return biodegradable items to the Earth by burying them.
- Toss into running water (again, only if biodegradable).
- Reuse after cleansing.
- Throw away any components you cannot dispose of more eco-consciously in a litter bin by a crossroads.

Baneful & Offensive Magick

MORTEM
OCCULTUS

It's Not Black or White – It Just Is

CALLING 'BAD' MAGICK black and 'good' magick white is antiquated and has racist origins. Magick is neither good nor evil – it simply is. Magick intended to cause harm is referred to as 'baneful' magick. There are three basic levels.

- **Jinx:** This creates a short streak of bad luck and usually involves only minor inconveniences.
- **Hex:** This is mean-spirited magick intended to cause a negative result. It's more intense than a jinx and usually done as revenge.
- **Curse:** A curse can create a long streak of misfortune that is more permanent and harder to remove. Breaking it may involve meeting a specific condition. It can be passed down through generations.

✷ LIFTING A JINX, HEX OR CURSE ✷

First, let's deal with what to do if you think you may have been hexed. There are various ways to lift a jinx, hex or curse.

Have I been hexed?

This is a traditional folk method of checking for a hex.

You will need: A bowl of room-temperature water and two matches.

- Bite the wooden ends off the matches.
- Strike both of the matches at the same time. When they burn out, toss them into the bowl of water, also at the same time.
- Wait ten minutes.
- Observe what shape the two matches form. Not touching = no hex. Touching = someone tried to hex you. Crossed = you've been successfully hexed.

Shower ritual to remove a jinx, hex or curse

- The rhyme I use is: 'May water cleanse me for my best. Here shall prosper no foul hex', but feel free to come up with your own. Modern rituals are just as effective, with the right intention behind them.
- Turn on the water and step into the shower.
- Stand beneath the stream and speak the phrase as many times as you feel you need to. While speaking, use soap or a salt scrub to cleanse yourself.
- Envision the hex washing off you as black sludge.
- Note: this probably won't break a generational curse, but doesn't hurt to try.

✷ URINE TO BREAK A HEX ✷

Yes, you read that correctly. This one is not for the faint of heart. Your urine, often called 'golden water', can be used to break a hex. That's right, you have permission to pee in the bath or shower (though if you do this, please rinse it off immediately you have finished).

Urine can also be used defensively. Urine contains your DNA and energetic signature.

Historically, witch bottles were made using urine and nine pins. These witch bottles were buried on the property, and were said to act as an energetic decoy to malicious spirits. They work by using your urine to trick negative energy into impaling itself on the pins.

Witch bottle recipe

Witch bottles can be used to deflect negative energy.

You will need: Urine, nine rusty nails/pins/needles, a glass bottle, spit, blood and/or fingernails.

- Combine the ingredients in the bottle.
- Seal the bottle, then bury it near your front door.

Delivering a Hex

Now it's time to give out! And the first thing you need is something to represent the subject of your hex.

✷ TAGLOCKS ✷

Taglocks direct the energy of a spell to a target. DNA is our essence, and the most potent taglock. It can be difficult nowadays to get hold of someone's blood, so below are some different taglock ideas.

- Hair.
- Fingernails.
- A picture of them.
- A piece of paper with their name and birthday.
- Anything they've touched.
- A personal item.
- Bodily fluids – semen is especially powerful.

Important note: always cover the top of your head when performing anything baneful. This can be with a veil, a hat, a hoodie, a blanket thrown over you or a headscarf or shawl. Don't let that energy anywhere near your crown.

Freezer spell

Someone bothering you, but not quite ready to do a full banishing ritual? Do a simple freezer spell, a binding ritual that freezes their energy, putting things on pause to deal with at your convenience (or leave them there forever – you do you).

You will need: Water (or vinegar for an extra-spicy spell), paper, a pen, a taglock (see left), a plastic bag, a jar or similar container (not glass, as frozen water can expand and crack the glass).

- Grab your taglock. Usually, a picture or a piece of paper with the person's full name and birthday is used for a freezer spell. Fold it away from you three times.
- Add your essence, either by licking the paper or spitting into the container.
- Fill your container with water (or vinegar, if they've really pissed you off), then put in your taglock. Shove it into the back of your freezer.
- Whenever you remember why they annoyed you, unfreeze and shake them up.

SPELLS & RECIPES

Recipes for Your Book of Shadows

For any spells and rituals, just remember: KISS – keep it simple, silly.

Witch's black salt recipe

Black salt is a common ingredient in spells. It can be used for protection, banishing or anywhere you need a little defensive salt. I don't use any particular proportions, just mix until it is a dark grey colour.

You will need: Salt and ash, black pepper and/or eggshell powder (optional).

- Mix together the ash and salt. Add some pepper and/or eggshell powder to achieve a dark grey mix.
- You can also stick incense upright in a container of salt so the ash naturally falls in for instant, easy, lazy-witch-approved black salt.

Eggshell powder

Which came first? The chicken, or witches using eggs in magick? In witchcraft, eggs symbolize fertility, rebirth, protection and transformation. Eggshells, made of calcium, have protective properties. If you're travelling somewhere with intense energy, draw crosses with this powder on the bottoms of your feet and the back of your neck.

You will need: Eggshells.

- Rinse your saved eggshells and store them in the fridge.
- To prepare the powder, put them in a pan of water and boil for ten minutes to sanitize, then drain and put in a roasting tin.

- Bake the shells in the oven at 105°C (222°F) for 22 minutes to dry.
- Using your mortar and pestle, grind the shells into powder, then rub through a fine sieve until you have a fine powder. Save any large pieces and mix into soil. Use this powder for protective purposes.

Rosemary oil recipe

Rosemary oil is the go-to of witchy oils – you can use it for anything as it combines the protective properties of rosemary and oil. Add it to a black candle for extra umph, or use it to anoint your protection braid before going out in public. When a working calls for a witchy oil, you can substitute rosemary oil with no ill-effects.

You will need: A few sprigs of rosemary, some neutral carrier oil (jojoba, grapeseed, almond) and a glass container.

- Rinse and dry the rosemary, then put it into a glass container. Fill the container with carrier oil, so it covers the rosemary. Put the lid on the container.
- Place on a sunny windowsill for about a month, shaking it when you remember, ideally every day. After a month, strain the oil and discard the rosemary sprigs. Pour the oil into a convenient bottle. Store somewhere cool and dry.

CORD-CUTTING

This is one of the most popular forms of purchased spellwork so today you are going to learn how to create a spell for yourself. Cord-cutting rituals are often employed to sever energetic ties, not necessarily ties between people. Try doing a cord-cutting for a place when you want to move, or a habit when you want to quit smoking. And the next time your bestie has a bad break-up, this will come in handy.

For a cord-cutting to be effective, you need to sever the string with something sharp; it is a common mistake not to pay attention to this. If you see candle cord-cuttings online, these are divination, not actual cord-cuttings. Not all spells need a candle. If you do not cut the string yourself, all you are doing is a reading, which is fine, but if your intention is to take a more active role, you need to cut the cord.

Cord-cutting spell

This spell will sever energetic ties. This cannot easily be undone, so only do it when you're super-serious about removing something from your life. If you're still vying to get back with that ex (which is almost ALWAYS a bad idea), don't do a cord-cutting. Put them in the freezer if you need a less permanent solution (page 141).

You will need: String, a picture of yourself, a picture or symbol of what you want to sever (a picture, a cigarette, etc) and a cutting tool, such as a boline.

- Roll the picture of the thing you want to sever away from you and tie it to one end of the cord. Roll the picture of yourself towards you and tie it to the other end of the cord.
- Take a moment to gather yourself and focus on the reasons why you want to sever this attachment. With a pair of scissors or your boline, cut the centre of the string. Burn the remains, if you wish.

HERBS FOR ABUNDANCE

Cinnamon, mint, catnip, spearmint, basil and rosemary are all potent herbs or spices to bring abundance into your life. Collect and dry the herbs, then add some cinnamon sticks and keep in a little bag (those little organza bags you get earrings in at Yuletide are ideal). Secure the bag with a few stitches or a ribbon and keep them in your purse, car or money corner.

Cinnamon coin abundance ritual

Cinnamon is a powerful (and delicious) spice, often used for abundance and success. For this simple ritual, all you need is cinnamon and a coin – any coin, in any currency, will work.

You will need: Ground cinnamon and a coin.

- On the first of the month, place the coin outside the front entrance of your home and sprinkle cinnamon over it.
- Pick up the cinnamon-covered coin with your left (or non-dominant) hand.
- Say the affirmation, 'I draw abundance, health, wealth and success to me effortlessly, without any blockages, for the good of all and with harm to none.'
- Blow the cinnamon off the coin and across the front threshold, into the home.
- Place the coin outside in front of the door overnight. Hide it if you need to, because it's not great luck if it gets stolen. Pick it up the next day and add it to your money bowl, or recirculate as usual.

Money bowl spell
Money that flows in without flowing out is indicative of a spiritual blockage, perhaps selfishness or cheapness. This spell will encourage you to be generous with your money and know it will always come back. Keep the bowl in your money corner (page 112).

You will need: A bowl or vessel, rice, salt, ground cinnamon (skip if you plan on composting),a candle and cash (coins or notes/bills), crystals or trinkets associated with money. Optional: *Honey and sugar.*

- Cleanse your space and cast a circle.
- Grab your vessel, or deconstruct your existing money bowl by removing and separating the ingredients. When breaking down an old money bowl, spend some of the cash to represent the flow of money. If there's any cinnamon on the notes (bills), wipe them down before recirculating, as cinnamon is a common allergen.
- Empty and clean the vessel. Then, clean it spiritually with smoke, sound or the medium of your choice.
- Add a base to the bowl. Some common bases are rice, honey, salt and sugar. If you are in an area with bugs, skip adding sugar or honey to your bowl. (Fun fact: cinnamon actually repels ants.) Don't skimp on the base, there needs to be enough to stick things in and keep them upright.
- Use your finger and swirl the herbs in with intention. Draw symbols or sigils into the rice while stirring. A plus sign, the infinity sign, or even a specific word you're trying to manifest are good options but go with your gut.
- Next, dress your candle however you'd like. Place in a candlestick holder in the centre. It may be tempting to put the candle directly in your base. Don't do this – fire safety concern. Never place a candle in anything unstable.
- Add the cash – the money part of the money bowl. You can place the notes (bills) in flat, or roll them. When rolling, always roll them towards you to draw in money. You can also rub cash with cinnamon to attract money quickly.

- Then comes the fun part. Add any crystals and trinkets you associate with money. Strategically place crystals that amplify, such as clear quartz, next to the highest value cash.
- When your bowl feels complete, light the candle to activate it. You can let the candle burn down all the way, or snuff it and burn it over a few days.
- Feed your money bowl through the month by adding bills and spare change. Refresh on the new moon.

Fast money spell

Cast this simple spell if you want to attract money quickly. Do this whenever you need a certain amount of money for a specific purpose.

You will need: A bay leaf and a green or gold pen.

- Write the amount you want to manifest on a bay leaf using the pen.
- Burn or bury the bay leaf.

Morning cinnamon ritual

With just some cinnamon and a dream, you too can add magick to your morning routine. I do this every day, and really notice if I skip it. Setting a clear intention sets you up for a successful day.

You will need: A mug, cinnamon, coffee or tea and a teaspoon.

- Sprinkle cinnamon into your morning coffee or tea.
- Speak your intention into the mug. Mine normally sounds something like, 'I am confident and powerful, and will achieve (add priority action) today. For the good of all and with harm to none, so mote it be.'
- Stir three times clockwise. Drink your beverage (well, what else would you do with it?).

INSTANT WITCH TIP – A shot of coffee

Add coffee grounds to any spell to speed things up.

Shop your pantry spell

The point of this spell is to prove you do not need to participate in capitalism to cast a spell effectively. Unless you are a committed minimalist, you probably have everything you need right in your cupboard. And who doesn't love shopping their closet? The only rule for this spell is to buy nothing.

You will need (as long as you don't buy them specially): A candle, herbs and oil.

- Set an intention for your spell. Find a candle: any candle, any colour. If you have no candles, no biggie.
- Go to your cupboard and select an odd number of herbs. Don't look up their correspondences.
- Pick one oil – cooking oils, like olive or sesame, work fine. Anoint the candle with the oil. Sprinkle on the herbs.
- Cast your circle.
- Make up a rhyme on the fly. That's right, we're practising our freestyling skill. It's okay if it's 'bad' or feels awkward. Light the candle and let it burn down all the way.
- Close the circle.
- Pat yourself on the back for using what you have.

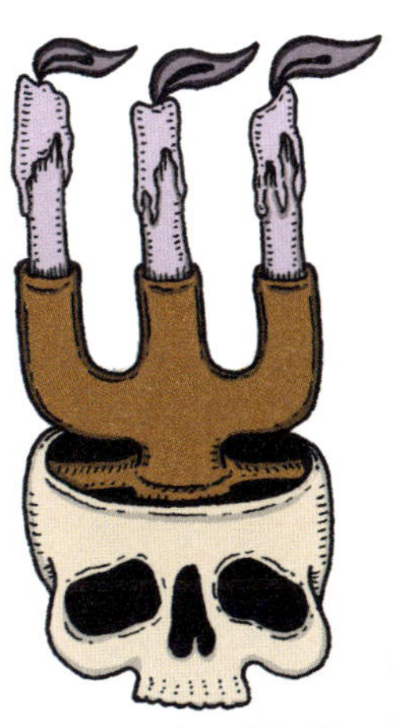

TO THE NEW WITCH, I WISH YOU LUCK.

SO MOTE IT BE.

Conclusion

Welcome to the endless pursuit of knowledge: knowing enough to realize you don't know much at all. You've learned the basics, travelled through the cycles of nature, and can spellcraft to your heart's content.

Being a witch is taking back your own power. Use your practice to become an active participant in your life. Shape your reality with your will and create the life of your dreams. We only get one try at this lifetime. Don't be afraid to experiment. Make mistakes. Use the 'wrong' herb. Hex your ex.

While we have reached the end of our journey together, I hope you continue on this crooked path. Thank you for coming along and for trusting me with your time. To the new witch, I wish you luck. So mote it be.

Glossary

Altar: A sacred space dedicated to magick and working with spirits.

Baneful magick: Magick performed with the intent to cause harm.

Circle: Cast before performing magick to separate a space from the mundane world.

Correspondence: Symbolic associations of an item's energy. Based on a variety of factors, and individual to each practitioner.

Crystal: Stones that form in a repeating pattern. Often aesthetically pleasing, used to direct and store energy.

Deity: A god or goddess.

Energy: The vital force that connects us all. What witches manipulate with magick.

Familiar: A spirit that comes to the aid of a witch, often in animal form.

Herb: The leafy or flowery parts of plants, typically dried.

Hex: A baneful working meant to inflict harm.

Magick: The art of shaping reality to one's will, using unseen forces.

Pagan: A broad term for non-Abrahamic religions. Normally polytheistic and nature based.

Sabbat: A pagan holiday. The eight celebrations that make up the wheel of the year.

Spell: A ritual action done with intent to achieve a result.

Spiritual cleansing: Cleaning performed to remove negative energy. Performed after cleaning normally.

Taglock: An item, often containing DNA, used to form a link between a target and a spell.

Tarot: A deck of cards used for fortune telling and divination.

Wicca: An Earth-based religion that embraces magick, founded in the mid 1900s.

ACKNOWLEDGEMENTS

BLESSED BE, WE'RE at the end. If you've made it this far, thank you. Thank you for your time, and for trusting me with your practice.

A huge thanks to my editor Phoebe, for gently guiding me through this process. I would not have finished this without you. To Mira, for bringing this book to life with your stunning illustrations. Shout out to the team at Quadrille: Claire, Wendy, and anyone else who worked on this book.

Thank you to my mom and dad, for nurturing my curiosity and never questioning my odd hobbies. A big thanks to Jordan, for supporting and loving me fully. I would've spiralled a million (more) times without your encouragement. Finally, to my familiars, Oz and Ku. Your little snoots get me up in the morning.

To all the witches who came before, and to those who follow.

ABOUT THE AUTHOR

Megan Archer's mission is simple: to make witchcraft more accessible, no matter where or how you live your life, while adapting it to modern times. Having grown up in Virginia with a fascination for the occult sparked by her dad teaching her tarot from a young age, Megan committed to expanding her witchcraft arsenal in 2019. Over the past six years, she has increased her knowledge and expertise and now teaches her own practices on social media. She's amassed a vast, engaged following from all around the world, focusing on beginner witch tips, house witch advice and spells and tricks. Her magickal practice fuses both Eurocentric and Asian spirituality – a nod to Megan's heritage. *INSTANT WITCH: The Beginner's Guide* is her first book.

INDEX

Quadrille, Penguin Random House UK,
One Embassy Gardens, 8 Viaduct Gardens,
London SW11 7BW

Quadrille Publishing Limited is part of the Penguin Random House group of companies whose addresses can be found at global.penguinrandomhouse.com

Published by Quadrille in 2025

www.penguin.co.uk

A CIP catalogue record for this book is available from the British Library

ISBN 978-1-83783-438-9
10 9 8 7 6 5 4 3 2 1

Managing Director: Sarah Lavelle
Publishing Director: Kate Pollard
Commissioning Editor: Phoebe Bath
Copyeditor: Wendy Hobson
Design: Claire Warner Studio
Illustrator: Mira Nurdianti
Senior Production Controller:
Martina Georgieva

Colour reproduction by p2d

Printed in China by RR Donnelley Asia Printing Solution Limited

The authorised representative in the EEA is Penguin Random House Ireland, Morrison Chambers, 32 Nassau Street, Dublin D02 YH68.

Penguin Random House is committed to a sustainable future for our business, our readers and our planet. This book is made from Forest Stewardship Council® certified paper.